An Inca Account of the Conquest of Peru

by Titu Cusi Yupanqui

An Inca Account of the Conquest of Peru
by Titu Cusi Yupanqui

TRANSLATED, INTRODUCED, AND ANNOTATED BY
Ralph Bauer

UNIVERSITY PRESS OF COLORADO

Published by the University Press of Colorado
5589 Arapahoe Avenue, Suite 206C
Boulder, Colorado 80303

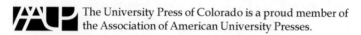 The University Press of Colorado is a proud member of
the Association of American University Presses.

The University Press of Colorado is a cooperative publishing enterprise supported, in part, by Adams State College, Colorado State University, Fort Lewis College, Mesa State College, Metropolitan State College of Denver, University of Colorado, University of Northern Colorado, and Western State College of Colorado.

∞ The paper used in this publication meets the minimum requirements of the American National Standard for Information Sciences — Permanence of Paper for Printed Library Materials. ANSI Z39.48-1992

Library of Congress Cataloging-in-Publication Data

Yupangui, Diego de Castro, titu cussi, 16th cent.
  [Relación de la conquista del Perú. English]
  An Inca account of the Conquest of Peru / by titu cusi Yupanqui ; translated, introduced, and annotated by Ralph Bauer.
       p. cm.
  Includes bibliographical references and index.
  ISBN 0-87081-807-4 (hardcover : alk. paper) — ISBN 0-87081-821-X (pbk. : alk. paper)
  1. Peru — History — Conquest, 1522–1548. 2. Peru — History — 1548–1820. I. Bauer, Ralph. II. Title.
  F3442.Y85 2005
  985'.02 — dc22

                                                                    2005006829

Design by Daniel Pratt

CEH Co-winner of the 2005 Colorado Endowment for the Humanities Publication Prize The CEH Publication Prize annually supports publication of outstanding nonfiction works that have strong humanities content and that make an area of humanities research more available to the Colorado public. The CEH Publication Prize funds are shared by the University Press of Colorado and the authors of the works being recognized. The Colorado Endowment for the Humanities is a state-wide, nonprofit organization dedicated to improving the quality of humanities education for all Coloradans.

For Grace

Contents

Illustrations

Acknowledgments

I would like to thank the staff of the Real Biblioteca del Monasterio San Lorenzo del Escorial, particularly José Luis del Valle Merino and Teodoro Alonso Turienzo, for permitting me to inspect the original manuscript of Titu Cusi's *Instrucción* and the staff of the Biblioteca del Palacio Real in Madrid, particularly Valentín Moreno and Pilar Uguiua, for their helpfulness in permitting me to produce a photocopy of the microfilm copy of the text. I also want to thank my colleague Regina Harrison for her patience and helpfulness in answering my questions. Thanks finally to K. Lane and the anonymous reader for University Press of Colorado for their invaluable comments, as well as to Darrin Pratt and Laura Furney for their patience and encouragement.

Chronology

ca. 1100	Manco Capac founds Cuzco
ca. 1438	Birth of Inca Urco
1438–1471	Life of Inca Pachacuti
1471–1493	Life of Topa Inca
1493	Birth of Huayna Capac
1521	Hernando Cortés conquers México-Tenochtitlan
1524	Death of Huayna Capac; partition of empire between Huascar and Atahuallpa
1530	Francisco Pizarro enters Inca territory
1532	Atahuallpa's victory over Huascar in civil war

1533 (January)	Pizarro captures Atahuallpa in Caxamarca
1533 (July)	Execution of Atahuallpa
1533 (July–November)	Coronation and death of Topa Huallpa
1533 (December)	Coronation of Manco Inca in Cuzco
1535	Francisco Pizarro founds Lima
1536	Siege of Cuzco by Manco Inca's forces
1537	Removal to Vilcabamba
1541 (July)	Assassination of Francisco Pizarro by loyalists of Diego de Almagro
1545	Assassination of Manco Inca; succession of Saire Topa
1546 (January)	Gonzalo Pizarro rebels against authority of the crown and assassinates the first viceroy of Peru, Blasco Núñez Vela
1551	Antonio de Mendoza is appointed second viceroy of Peru
1554	Petition of Peruvian encomenderos for perpetuity of the encomienda
1556	The emperor Charles V steps down; his son Philip II is crowned emperor
1556 (June)	Andrés Hurtado de Mendoza, Marquis of Cañete, is appointed third viceroy of Peru
1556 (October)	Saire Topa accepts Spanish proposal to give up residency at Vilcabamba and remove to Cuzco
1560	Death of Saire Topa in Cuzco
1560	Coronation of Titu Cusi Yupanqui in Vilcabamba
1561	Arrival of the Count of Nieva as fourth viceroy of Peru
1564	The licenciate García de Castro arrives in Lima as president of audiencia
1568	Titu Cusi is baptized at Vilcabamba

1569	Arrival of fifth viceroy of Peru, Francisco de Toledo
1570	Fray Marcos García, Diego Ortiz, and Martín de Pando arrive at Vilcabamba; redaction of Titu Cusi's account
1571	Death of Titu Cusi Yupanqui and succession of Topa Amaru
1572	Spanish invasion of Vilcabamba; execution of Topa Amaru on orders of viceroy Francisco de Toledo

An Inca Account of
the Conquest of Peru
by Titu Cusi Yupanqui

Introduction

From Cajamarca to Vilcabamba

The text presented here for the first time in full-length English translation is an account of the cataclysmic events that took place in the Andes during the sixteenth century.[1] Its author, Diego de Castro Titu Cusi Yupanqui (1530?–1571), was the penultimate descendant of the Inca dynasty. His grandfather was Huayna Capac (b. 1493), who once ruled a vast empire that stretched from South America's Pacific coastline eastward across the Andes into the Amazonian lowlands and from what is today southern Columbia southward into central Chile and Argentina—a distance roughly equal to that between New York and Los Angeles. Although the Incas had been a rather insignificant ethnic group who controlled little more than their ancestral homelands around Cuzco only a few generations before Huayna Capac's succession, he had inherited the largest polity that the Americas had seen.[2] His empire was called the Tahuantinsuyu ("the parts that in their fourness make up the whole") because it was composed of four major geographical quarters — the Chinchaysuyu in the northwest, the Antisuyu in the northeast, the Cuntisuyu in the southwest, and the Collasuyu in the southeast (see Illustration 1). These vast territories included scores of other tributary ethnic groups and were connected by a road system whose major highways covered some 25,000 miles — a distance approximately equal to the circumference of the earth. Huayna Capac had just brought under his dominion the northern kingdom of Quito, where he reportedly planned to found a second capital city, when, in 1524, he was informed of the appearance of bearded white strangers, who claimed to have arrived "by the wind" on the northwestern coast of the empire.[3] Soon after receiving this news, his army and court were struck by a violent disease that killed thousands, including Huayna Capac and his presumptive heir, Ninan Coyoche, probably in 1526. The epidemic that killed Huayna Capac and his heir was probably smallpox, which had been brought by the Spanish explorers and conquerors from Europe. It had rapidly spread around the Caribbean, Mexico, Central America, and down into South America, killing tens of thousands of Native Americans, who had no biological resistance.

The bearded white strangers who were reported to have landed on the northwestern coast were a band of eighty Spaniards under the leadership of Francisco Pizarro (b. 1471), a hidalgo (petty gentleman) from Trujillo in Extremadura.[4] He had come to the New World in 1509, participated in Vasco Núñez de Balboa's expedition resulting in the European discovery of the Pacific Ocean in 1513, and subsequently established himself as a colonist living on Native labor in Panama. Inspired by the fabulous exploits of Hernando Cortés in the conquest of Mexico (1520), Pizarro had

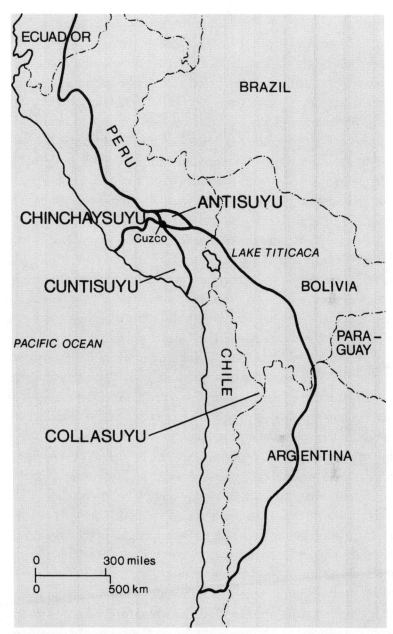

1. *Map of Tahuantinsuyu.* From Moseley, The Incas and Their Ancestors: The Archaeology of Peru *(London: Thames & Hudson, 1991 and 2001), 24. Reprinted by kind permission of Michael Moseley and Thames & Hudson*

entered into partnership with another citizen of Panama, Diego de Almagro, and a priest by the name of Hernando de Luque in order to explore the South American coastline and search for his own Mexico. Although their first expedition ended in failure in 1524, they found many signs of a great civilization during their coastal exploration. More expeditions were mounted and in 1530 a band of approximately 160 Spaniards landed on the Ecuadorian coast under Pizarro's command and made their push inland. The Spaniards, however, found the land in devastation—the result, as they learned from the Natives, of a tremendous civil war that had been ravaging the entire country.

The civil war was the consequence of the untimely deaths of Huayna Capac and his heir, which had left the two eldest of his seven surviving sons fighting for succession to the Inca throne.[5] Huascar was initially crowned by the Inca nobility of Cuzco and controlled the southern parts of Tahuantinsuyu. His succession was challenged, however, by his half-brother Atahuallpa, who controlled the northern territories surrounding Quito and had the loyalty of Huayna Capac's most able generals and their armies. When Huascar rejected Atahuallpa's proposals for a peaceful arrangement, a deadly struggle ensued between the northern and southern parts of the empire. Huascar initially appeared to have the upper hand, even capturing his half-brother. But Atahuallpa was able to make his escape, and soon the tide turned, partially because of Huascar's unpopularity among his own officers. In a major battle outside Cuzco Atahuallpa's general Quisquis defeated Huascar's forces, took Huascar prisoner, captured the capital, and, on Atahuallpa's orders, had the Inca nobility loyal to Huascar persecuted and murdered (see Illustration 2).

It was in the immediate aftermath of these turbulent events that the Spaniards appeared on the scene in Peru and first met with the victorious Atahuallpa at the northern town of Cajamarca on 16 November 1532 (see Illustration 3). The Spaniards came to the meeting with a plan, well tried in the conquest of Mexico, of

2. *Huascar Inca (the Twelfth Inca) is taken prisoner by Atahuallpa's generals. From Felipe Guaman Poma de Ayala,* Nueva corónica y buen gobierno. *By kind permission of the Royal Library at Copenhagen (GKS 2232 4to), which owns the original manuscript and has published the full facsimile and a transcription on-line at http://www.kb.dk/elib/mss/poma/index-en.htm*

taking the enemy leader hostage and using him as a puppet to control his subjects and extort gold and silver. Atahuallpa, under-estimating the small band of strangers, left behind the greater part of his army, at least forty thousand strong, and came to the meeting in the enclosed main square of Cajamarca accompanied by only a lightly armed contingent of five or six thousand men. There he was ambushed by the Spaniards, who wreaked havoc among the terrified Andean warriors with arquebuses, cannons, and cavalry. The Spaniards killed at least 1,500 Andeans on that infamous day and took Atahuallpa prisoner without suffering a single casualty.

Atahuallpa, now in captivity and fearful that Huascar might try to take advantage of the situation by aligning himself with the strangers, gave orders to have his brother murdered. After Huascar's death, Atahuallpa attempted to ransom himself by paying the Spaniards an enormous treasure of precious objects, which the Spaniards melted down to more than eleven tons in gold and thirteen tons in silver. Atahuallpa, despite Spanish prom-ises, was not released and ruled the country from his captivity for half a year before he was finally garroted by his captors in July 1533 (see Illustration 4).[6]

With both warring contenders for the Inca royal tassel dead and the Spaniards greedy for more gold, the conquerors marched on Cuzco. En route they were engaged in several fierce battles by the warriors of Atahuallpa's general Quisquis but received a friendly reception from Atahuallpa's enemies, both among the Inca nobility of Cuzco and among other ethnic groups who had been loyal to Huascar in the civil war.[7] As a result, the Spaniards succeeded in capturing the Inca capital on Saturday, 15 Novem-ber 1533. Eager for a new puppet-Inca who would exercise con-trol on their behalf, the Spaniards proclaimed Atahuallpa's and Huascar's younger brother Topa Huallpa as the successor to the crown. When Topa Huallpa suddenly died en route to Cuzco in December 1533, Francisco Pizarro crowned their brother Manco

3. *Atahuallpa meets Francisco Pizarro, the priest Vicente de Valverde, and their translator Felipillo. From Guaman Poma de Ayala,* Nueva corónica y buen gobierno. *By kind permission of the Royal Library at Copenhagen (GKS 2232 4to)*

4. *Atahuallpa is executed by the Spaniards. From Guaman Poma de Ayala,* Nueva corónica y buen gobierno. *By kind permission of the Royal Library at Copenhagen (GKS 2232 4to)*

Inca, who had lived in Cuzco and had still been an adolescent during the Inca civil war between his two older half-brothers Atahuallpa and Huascar.

Initially, Manco Inca collaborated with the Spaniards in the ongoing fight against Atahuallpa's generals. As the Spaniards' greed and treatment of Manco Inca became increasingly intolerable, however, the old divisions between the loyalists of Atahuallpa and Huascar gave way to a shared resentment of the Spanish invaders. In 1536 Manco Inca fled Cuzco in order to take command of an enormous army of 100,000 warriors who had gathered outside the capital, ready to throw off the Spanish yoke. Under Manco Inca's command, the Native armies simultaneously besieged Cuzco and Lima, cutting off communications between the two Spanish strongholds.[8] Although they brought the Spaniards to the brink of disaster, even killing one of the Pizarro brothers, Juan, in the process, the effort ultimately failed, and the rebellious Andeans withdrew to the tropical lowlands of Vitcos and Vilcabamba on the eastern slopes of the Andes the following year (1537). In this remote refuge, Manco Inca re-created a neo-Inca state that resisted all Spanish incursions for more than thirty years, waging a guerrilla war on Spanish trade routes and towns as well as neighboring ethnic groups subjected to Spanish rule.[9]

With Manco Inca defiant and out of their control, the Spaniards in Cuzco crowned another of Huayna Capac's sons as their new puppet ruler—Paullu Topa (1518–1549), who had remained loyal to the Spaniards during the siege of Cuzco and continued to assist with their numerous attempts to quell the resistance of the neo-Inca state at Vilcabamba. Now, however, the Spaniards were falling out amongst each other. Whereas Pizarro's men had become fabulously rich in the extortion of Atahuallpa's ransom at Cajamarca, the men of Almagro's party, who had not been in Cajamarca at that time, had received only small portions. This caused deep resentment between the pizarrista and almagrista factions and escalated into a fierce struggle from which Pizarro emerged victorious. In 1538 Almagro was executed by one of Pizarro's brothers, Hernando, after having lost the decisive battle of Las Salinas outside Cuzco. Almagro's death did not, however, end the hostilities between the two factions. In July 1541 Francisco Pizarro was assassinated by Almagro's son, who proclaimed himself governor but was later condemned to death by the official governor sent by the Crown in order to settle the dispute. The chaos in Spanish-controlled Peru was further aggravated when the youngest of the Pizarros, Gonzalo, rebelled against the authority of the first viceroy sent by the Crown, Blasco Núñez Vela. Although the insurgent initially was victorious against the royalist army in the battle of Añaquito (1546), in which the viceroy Núñez Vela was killed, Gonzalo Pizarro was finally defeated and executed in 1548 by an army loyal to the Crown led by the new royal governor Pedro de la Gasca.[10]

Manco Inca had observed these wars among the Spaniards from his remote outpost at Vilcabamba with great interest, providing occasional help to the weaker almagrista faction in the hope that the Spaniards would ultimately destroy, or at least significantly weaken, one another. After he had granted refuge, however, to some Spaniards who had been on the run for their role in Francisco Pizarro's assassination, in 1545 he was treacherously murdered by his Spanish guests, who might have been instigated to do this in exchange for Spanish officials' assurances of clemency in regard to their murder of Pizarro (Hemming, 276). Upon his death, Manco Inca left his oldest son, Saire Topa, as his successor. But Saire Topa was seen as a weak leader by the Inca nobles in Vilcabamba and in 1556 he moved to Cuzco to live under Spanish rule, accepting an offer of a repartimiento (an allotment of land and Native tributaries) from viceroy Andrés Hurtado de Mendoza. After Saire Topa's departure, his half brother Titu Cusi Yupanqui, author of the text translated here, was left in charge of Vilcabamba. When news of Saire Topa's sudden death arrived from Cuzco four years later,[11] Titu Cusi was officially crowned

Inca. Through shrewd politics of resistance and negotiation, Titu Cusi was able to maintain the independence of the neo-Inca state at Vilcabamba for another decade. He died under mysterious circumstances (probably from pneumonia) in 1571, leaving his younger brother, Topa Amaru, in charge of Vilcabamba. In 1572 a Spanish army sent by the new viceroy, Francisco de Toledo, succeeded in invading Vilcabamba and in capturing Topa Amaru. Topa Amaru's subsequent execution on the main square of Cuzco marked the end of the neo-Inca state at Vilcabamba and of the paternal line of the Inca dynasty. Andean resistance against the Spanish invaders, however, continued. Even two hundred years later, major Native rebellions shook Peru, instigated by leaders who claimed descent from the Incas by the maternal line — such as Juan Santos Atahuallpa in the 1760s and José Gabriel Condorcanqui Topa Amaru II in the 1780s.[12] Even to this day, the Incas' imperial legacy is frequently appropriated by Peruvian resistance fighters who violently reject the neo-European social order of the American nation states.

Titu Cusi's Hybrid Account of the Conquest of Peru

The brief summary of the main historical battles and events of the Conquest of Peru above conveys a sense of the extraordinary violence at the foundation of European empires and American nation states in the New World. It cannot do justice, however, to the whole story of Andean resistance and survival. Aware that their clubs, pikes, and slingshots were largely ineffective against the armored and mounted Spanish conquistadors, Native leaders soon learned to appropriate not only the foreigners' use of swords, firearms, and horses but also the most powerful weapon that the invaders had brought: the written word. The text presented here tells an early chapter in the long history of Native appropriation of this European medium. It tells the story of the Conquest of Peru not from the familiar perspective of the Spanish conquerors but from the perspective of one of the main actors in the Andean resistance to the European colonial order.[13] The year before his death in 1571, Titu Cusi related his story to an Augustinian missionary then at residence at Vilcabamba, fray Marcos García, so that his His Majesty, King Philip II, may be enlightened "with regard to the manner and times in which the Spaniards intruded into these lands of Peru and of the way they treated my father while he was still alive before they killed him in this land, which is now mine" (see p. 59). He related his story in the Inca language, Quechua, while the Spanish missionary "ordered" and translated it into Spanish. Marcos García's translation was then transcribed by Titu Cusi's mestizo secretary, Martín de Pando. The manuscript, completed on 6 February 1570, survives today in the royal library of the Monastery of the Escorial, Philip II's monastic refuge outside Madrid. It is one of the most fascinating documents preserved from sixteenth-century Peru, telling the story of continuing Native cultural resistance, change, mixture, and survival in the Americas after the European invasion.

Titu Cusi—whose name means "the Magnanimous and Fortunate"—was born around 1530 in Cuzco and lived there until his father's removal to Vilcabamba. When he was about seven years old, he was captured from Vilcabamba during a Spanish raid and taken to Cuzco to be brought up in the house of Pedro de Oñate. Oñate seems to have been on overall good terms with Manco Inca, for Titu Cusi relates that "[w]hen my father found out about this, he sent a messenger to Oñate in order to thank him and officially to put me and my two sisters into his care, asking him to look after me and them and promising that he would show his gratitude" (p. 118). Titu Cusi's reference to his patron as "a so-and-so Oñate," however, also suggests that his stay with Oñate left little impression on him.

It is uncertain how much Spanish Titu Cusi learned during his captivity in Cuzco. In general, it was rare for the Inca nobility of Cuzco to know Spanish during this early period of Spanish colonialism in Peru. Even Titu Cusi's uncle Paullu — who had sided with the Spaniards at every opportunity, received a repartimiento from Pizarro, lived among Spaniards in Cuzco, worn Spanish clothes, and even participated in Spanish military expeditions in distant Chile — could not speak, read, or write Spanish, save for signing his name. Because this repeatedly made him the prey of Spanish ruffians who took advantage of his language barrier, in 1541 the authorities found it necessary to enact a royal decree giving him a Spanish tutor to look after his interests and prevent him from signing dubious contracts (see Hemming, 258–259). Although Paullu's son Carlos (Titu Cusi's cousin) was educated in a Spanish school and did learn to speak Spanish (as well as Latin), later even marrying a Spanish woman (Julien, 44; Hemming, 341), the acquisition of the Castilian language by Natives remained generally a controversial subject throughout the sixteenth century among the various sectors of Spanish society (see Mannheim, 61–109; Andrien, 106–119). On the one hand, the conquerors and their settler descendants had, as Bruce Mannheim points out, a "stake in ensuring that native populations continue to speak a Native Andean language rather than Spanish," for they were able to manipulate the language barrier to their advantage in legal disputes (Mannheim, 108). Many among the clergy as well promoted Quechua, rather than Spanish, as the lingua franca, recognizing the pragmatic advantages of making use of Quechua for administrative and proselytizing purposes.[14] The first three Provincial Councils of Lima (1551–1583) therefore encouraged the writing of catechisms and the formal training of missionaries in Quechua. It was in this context that the first Quechua grammar book and dictionary were produced by fray Domingo de Santo Tomás in 1560 (to which we will return later). On the other hand, Hispanization was generally the preferred policy of the Crown and some sectors of the clergy, who were concerned about the purity of Christian religious concepts once translated into Quechua. Although the balance would tip in favor of Hispanization by the end of the sixteenth century, during the time that Titu Cusi spent in Cuzco (1537–1542) it would not have been taken for granted that the offspring of the Inca nobility learn Spanish. But even if Titu Cusi had learned some Spanish during his captivity as a child, it is highly unlikely that he would have used it much during the nearly thirty years that would pass before he related his account in Quechua to García Marcos. Unlike his cousin Carlos, Titu Cusi spent virtually the entire period at Vilcabamba, where no or only little Spanish would have been spoken.

By his own account, Titu Cusi returned to Vilcabamba after he was abducted from Cuzco by his father's messengers. If we give credence to his statement that he rejoined his father in Vitcos around the time of the arrival of the Spanish refugees who would later murder Manco Inca, his return would have occurred around 1542 when he was about twelve years old. During the "many days" (p. 125) he then spent with his father at Vilcabamba (probably only about three years), he was able to observe Manco Inca's style of governing the rebellious neo-Inca outpost. Once Titu Cusi was in charge of Vilcabamba after his father's death in 1545 and his brother's departure in 1556, he carried on his father's resistance against Spanish authority.

The period of his reign, however, also saw several overtures toward peaceful accommodation. In part, this was the result of a change in Spanish policy and leadership. In 1564 the Crown had sent a provisional governor general and president of the Council at Lima, Lope García de Castro, in order to take charge of the government until a new viceroy should be appointed. (The previous viceroy, Diego López de Zuñiga, Count of Nieva, had died unexpectedly earlier that year.) Meanwhile, Spanish authorities were becoming increasingly concerned about the growing support that nativist resistance movements were receiving among many of the already "pacified" indigenous population. Earlier that year, for example, a Spanish priest, Luis de Olvera, had discovered alarming news about a rapidly spreading millenarian movement, called Taqui Qnqoy, whose leaders called for an outright rejection of Christianity and all things European as well as for a return to the ancient *huacas* (sacred objects or spaces).[15] Although the movement was eventually put down by Spanish authorities, García de Castro pursued a reconciliatory and diplomatic approach to the problem still posed by the rebels at Vilcabamba. Titu Cusi reciprocated the demonstrations of goodwill by frequently exchanging letters with Spanish authorities in Lima and Cuzco, entertaining Spanish missionaries in his refuge, and even allowing himself to be baptized and adopting a Christian name — Diego de Castro, in honor of the Spanish governor. A meeting was arranged at the bridge of Chuquichaca with the *oidor* (judge) of the Audiencia of Charcas, Juán de Matienzo, in order to negotiate the terms under which Titu Cusi would receive a substantial repartimiento in exchange for giving up his refuge. Moreover, it was agreed that Titu Cusi's son, Quispe Titu, would marry Saire Topa's daughter, christened as Beatriz, who lived in Cuzco and was heir to a substantial estate. In order to negotiate the terms of this arrangement, gifts, promises, messages, and official letters were exchanged, including the present text. Ultimately, however, nothing came of these negotiations and Titu Cusi, unlike his brother Saire Topa, remained in Vilcabamba.

Some historians have interpreted Titu Cusi's conversion to Christianity as more of a diplomatic ploy than an action motivated by true religious conviction while others have seen it as generally sincere (see Kubler; Hemming, 336, respectively). Although it is impossible to know with certainty what motivated Titu Cusi to convert, it is significant that despite allowing Christian missionaries to erect a large cross and to preach at Vilcabamba, repeatedly shielding them against some of the outspoken enemies of Christianity among his followers and professing his own admiration for missionaries and their apostolic message (see p. 133), he never allowed Christian monotheism to supplant the Incas'

practice of sun worship or of paying homage to their multitudi-
nous huacas. It is also telling that his relationship with Marcos
García sharply deteriorated when the Augustinian, who seems
to have been somewhat rigid and inflexible, insisted on ending
the ancient Inca custom of polygamy. Indeed, not long after the
completion of Titu Cusi's account, Marcos García was expelled
from Vilcabamba, leaving behind his Augustinian brother Diego
Ortiz. In the long run, his expulsion turned out to be lucky for
Marcos García. When in 1571 Titu Cusi suddenly fell ill and died
within a few days, the Vilcabamba Incas blamed Ortiz and demanded that he resuscitate their leader. He failed, however, to
accomplish this feat, and so the enraged Andeans killed both
Ortiz and Pando after subjecting the former to an extended and
cruel martyrdom.[16] The missionary's death was subsequently used
to justify the invasion of Vilcabamba and the execution of Topa
Amaru (see Ocampo 215–216).

There is also a question about the sincerity of Titu Cusi's
negotiations with Spanish authorities regarding his departure
from Vilcabamba. These overtures, like his conversion, may well
have been a diplomatic delay tactic intended to keep the Spaniards at bay through demonstrations of goodwill while adroitly
evading all real changes to the status quo.[17] Even though in his
narrative Titu Cusi complained about "the hardships I suffer in
these jungles as a result of His Majesty's and His vassals' having
taken possession of this land" (p. 58), a return to Cuzco would
have put him and his followers at the mercy of the Spaniards.[18]
Previous experiences with the Spanish intruders could hardly have
inspired him with confidence in this regard. Moreover, he may
well have remembered the words of his father, who, as Titu Cusi
relates, had exhorted him and his followers "never to deal with
people like these, so you won't end up like me" (p. 127) and to
"pretend on the outside that you agree to their demands. . . . But
never forget our own ceremonies" (p. 116). Even though Titu
Cusi was generally tolerant of Spanish culture, he, unlike his uncle

Paullu and cousin Carlos, continued the traditional Inca ways of life. A contemporary Spaniard who had met him, Diego de Rodíguez de Figueroa, described him as wearing full ceremonial custom, including a "multicolored headdress, a diadem on his forehead and another one on his neck, a colored mask, a silver plate on his chest, garters of feathers, and carrying a golden lance, dagger, and shield" (see Hemming, 314). Unwilling to submit to the Spanish yoke but knowing that Vilcabamba was not strong enough to withstand a concerted Spanish assault, Titu Cusi walked a fine line between resistance and accommodation in his attempt to preserve his refuge. For example, he strictly forbade the admittance of any Spanish settlers (apart from the missionaries) into the valley in order to avoid conflicts that might provoke Spanish military action. The early seventeenth-century chronicler Antonio de Calancha relates that when in 1570 a sole Spanish prospector turned up at Vilcabamba to ask for permission to search for gold in the area, Titu Cusi acquiesced assuming that there was none to be found. When, contrary to Titu Cusi's expectations, the Spaniard did find gold and brought it to Titu Cusi thinking "that the Inca would be delighted" and grant him a new license for more exploration, Titu Cusi had the man killed and thrown into a river so not to "arouse the greed and attract thousands of Spaniards" (quoted in Hemming, 337).

These events tell us much about the reasons why Titu Cusi decided to have his story translated and transcribed for a Spanish audience and about the poetics of the surviving text. Some critics have suggested that such a decision seems to privilege European alphabetical writing over indigenous structures of knowledge—such as Andean oral traditions or the *quipu* (the records the Incas kept by way of colored knots)—and to betray a Eurocentric perspective that may have originated either with Titu Cusi's own acceptance of imposed European cultural norms or with a manipulation by the Spanish translator (see Luiselli, 30, n.1). Although this is probably a reasonable inference to make with regard to fray Marcos García, it would be unwarranted with regard to Titu Cusi. Rather, I would argue that his choice of the written medium must be seen in the context of the overall rhetorical nature of this text as a pragmatic attempt at intercultural diplomacy. When addressing a European monarch and court, Titu Cusi's history had to bridge a considerable hermeneutic gap. For this reason, Frank Salomon has called Native American chronicles, such as Titu Cusi's account, "Chronicles of the Impossible" — diachronic narratives of the conquest era that must be fully intelligible to Spanish contemporaries and at the same time made from and faithful to Andean materials alien to European diachrony (Salomon 1982, 9). Titu Cusi made hereby calculated use of everything he had learned about Spanish culture without becoming unfaithful to his own culture. His rhetorical strategy included his choice not only of the written medium but also of the Augustinian Marcos García as his translator and mouthpiece. Indeed, Marcos García was chosen after Titu Cusi had made inquiries (as he tells us in his narrative), asking "who among the monks in Cuzco was the most outstanding personality and which religion enjoyed the widest approbation and power" and after having learned that "the mightiest, most respected, and most flourishing religion was that of the Lord St. Augustine" (p. 133).

Titu Cusi understood the importance of alphabetical writing in dealing with the Spaniards. Thus, he relates that one of the reasons why the Andean people who first saw the Spaniards upon their arrival in Tahuantinsuyu called the strangers *Viracochas* (gods) was that "the Indians saw them alone talking to white cloths [*paños blancos*], as a person would speak to another, which is how the Indians perceived the reading of books and letters" (p. 60). Similarly memorable is Titu Cusi's account of the fateful encounter between the Spaniards and Atahuallpa at Cajamarca in 1532. He relates that the Spaniards "showed my uncle a letter or a book (I'm not sure exactly which), explaining to him that this was the word of God and of the king. My uncle . . . took the letter (or whatever it was) and threw it down, saying, 'What is this supposed to be that you gave to me here? Be gone!'" (p. 61). The subsequent Spanish attack was triggered when Atahuallpa, in a haughty gesture, flung the breviary presented to him by the priest Vicente de Valverde into the dust. The book contained the infamous *requirimiento* (Requirement), a text that by law had to be read aloud to the Natives and which informed them of their obligation to "acknowledge the Church as the Ruler and Superior of the whole world. . . . And the high priest called Pope, and in his name the King and the Queen" (quoted in Hanke, 33). Noncompliance was legitimate ground for the commencement of violent conquest. The power attributed to the written word in dealing with the Spaniards reverberates in many other Andean sources relating this scene and dating from the sixteenth century to the present, both written and oral.[19] Thus, Juan de Betanzos—a Spaniard who was married to Atahuallpa's sister (Francisco Pizarro's former mistress), Doña Angelina Yupanqui, who told the story of the Conquest as remembered by her family—wrote that, after the interpreter had explained to Atahuallpa that he should "obey the captain [Pizarro] who was also the son of the Sun, and that was what . . . the painting in the book said," Atahuallpa "asked for the book and, taking it in his hands he opened it. When he saw the lines of letters, he said, 'This speaks and says that you are the son of the Sun? I, also, am the son of the Sun' . . . Saying this, he hurled the book away" (Betanzos, 263). Similarly, the indigenous Andean chronicler Guaman Poma de Ayala, writing during the early seventeenth century, remembers Atahuallpa's response to the book like this: "'Give me the book so that it can speak to me.' And so he [Valverde] gave it to him and he held it in his hands and began to inspect the pages of the said book. And then the Inca said, 'Why doesn't it speak to me?'" before angrily throwing it to the ground (Guaman Poma, 357). Once in captivity, Atahuallpa reportedly asked the Spaniards to be taught how to "listen" to these texts. Finally, the early seventeenth-century *Huarochirí Manuscript,* written by an anonymous Andean probably recruited by the Spanish priest Francisco de Avila, begins by stating, "If the ancestors of the people called Indians had known writing in former times, then the lives they lived would not have faded from view until now. As the mighty past of the Spanish Vira Cochas is visible until now, So too would theirs be" (*Huarochirí Manuscript,* 41).

Constance Classen has argued that what made writing so "radically novel" for the Incas was its "disembodied nature." Unlike the Native non-alphabetical quipu, which still required oral transmission, European writing represented and appeared to act as a "substitute of speech," thus placing knowledge outside the human body (Classen, 127). But although this might be true for Atahuallpa and the first Andeans who came in contact with Europeans, it is unlikely that Titu Cusi (whom she cites here) would have viewed writing as radically novel, having lived in Cuzco and, in fact, now (in 1570) making use of it by relating his story for translation and transcription. Atahuallpa's successors quickly learned to use the written word for political purposes in dealing with the Spaniards, employing scribes and even becoming themselves literate in the foreign medium. Although Titu Cusi doubtlessly understood the power of alphabetical writing in Spanish culture, there is little evidence suggesting that he believed it inherently superior to Andean practices of recording and memorizing the past or even thought of it as divine. His own explanation of his decision to have his narrative written down—that "[since] the memory of men is frail and weak, it would be impossible to remember everything accurately with regard to all our great and important affairs unless we avail ourselves of writing [letras] to assist us in our purposes" (p. 58)—may well contain a hint of irony. After all, native Andeans *did* remember their own histories without alphabetical writing. Indeed, Titu Cusi was himself drawing on these non-alphabetical traditions even as he spoke when relating his account to fray Marcos García. Thus, we may read Titu Cusi's reference to the men whose memory is frail and weak unless assisted by writing not so much as a general statement about humanity's shortcomings at large but rather as a critical commentary specifically on Spanish infidelities to the spoken word.

The composition of this text was profoundly informed by Spanish and native Andean structures of knowledge, fusing various and often incommensurate rhetorical practices and conceptions of history. Related orally in Quechua by a speaker known to be curious about the culture of his Spanish audience, translated by a Spanish missionary whose knowledge of Quechua was probably proficient though limited, and transcribed from an oral medium into a written one by a bilingual mestizo, this text is an apt expression of the hybrid culture that was taking shape in sixteenth-century colonial Peru and resulting from some forty years of intercultural contact, conflict, and mixture.[20] It was a colonial culture, to be sure, whose intercultural exchanges occurred under conditions of extreme power imbalances. Nevertheless, it was a culture that was neither entirely Spanish nor entirely Andean but had become, as various historians and anthropologists have put it, "mutually entangled."[21]

On the one hand, Native leaders quickly learned not only that writing was the foundation for European notions of truth in general but also that it was particularly closely tied to royal power. After their battle-axes had failed them against the Spanish conquerors, many of whom (like Francisco Pizarro himself) were illiterate or only marginally literate (see Lockhart 1972, 135–156), here might yet be an effective weapon in the fight against the Spaniards' claims of being the new rightful lords of Peru. It was with this awareness that many Latin American Indian chronicles, such as that of Titu Cusi as well as those of Felipe Guaman Poma de Ayala (1615) and Juan de Santacruz Pachacuti Yamqui (1613) were written. As Angel Rama has argued, if writing had already been a privileged medium in Spanish culture before the American conquests, it "took on an almost sacred aura" in the largely illiterate territories of the New World (9–10). It is in this context of a culture of "letrados" — what Rama calls the "lettered city" — emerging in the Spanish empire that Titu Cusi's instructions to Marcos García and Martín de Pando with regard to his narrative must be seen: "[Because] I am unfamiliar with the phrases and modes of expression used by the Spaniards in such writings—[I] have asked the reverend fray don Marcos García and the secretary Martín de Pando to arrange and compose the said account in their customary ways of expression" (p. 136).

Formally, the text is divided into three distinct major sections: (1) a short introductory part explicitly addressed to Lope García de Castro, the departing governor of Peru, with Titu Cusi's request (*instrucción*) to present his text to King Philip II; (2) Titu Cusi's historical account (*relación*) of the Spanish Conquest of Peru, his father's maltreatment at the hands of the conquerors, the ensuing military conflicts, his father's withdrawal to Vilcabamba, his eventual murder there, and Titu Cusi's own succession as Inca, as well as his conversion to Christianity, leading up to the production of the manuscript; and (3) a power of attorney (*poder*) in which Titu Cusi authorizes García de Castro to represent him legally in the courts of Spain in any matter pertaining to his interests, title, or possessions.

Most likely, this surface structure of the text must be ascribed to the "ordering" hand of the translator fray Marcos García. The text's generic designations help us reconstruct the Spanish cultural context in which Titu Cusi's account of the Conquest of Peru must be seen. In early modern Spain, the designation of a text as a *relación* identified it as belonging to a genre that originated, as Roberto González Echevarría has shown, in legal discourse, especially notarial rhetoric, denoting an eyewitness account in a legal dispute. A defining characteristic of the relación genre, as it originated in the Old World context, was its humble, plain, but highly official character, as well as its appeal to the authority of firsthand experience.[22] In the New World context of overseas expansionism during the sixteenth century, however, the term relación took on a new meaning, now becoming, as Walter Mignolo has shown, largely synonymous with the terms *historia* (history) and *crónica* (chronicle), "in order to refer to a historiographic text."[23] In the context of overseas imperialism, law and history became inextricably intertwined. One of the most common subgenres of the relación was hereby the *relación de méritos* (the account of merits). These were personal narratives composed not for a *public* audience in the modern sense of the word but rather for a patrimonial audience within the hierarchy of the monarchical state in order to supplicate the monarch for a royal pension, office, or favors as compensation for services rendered to the Crown. Their printing was frequently paid for by the author himself, making this type of writing "one of the major genres of publishing in colonial Spanish America" (MacLeod, 1). As González Echevarría points out, "many of the adventures and misadventures, by people who were marginal to society, found their way to legal or quasi-legal documents in which lives large and small were told in search of acquittal or social advancement" (1980, 20–21). Nevertheless, the vast majority of these texts remained unpublished and survive today only in manuscript form. Typically, their publication was patronized by the Crown only if they contained material that was of wider interest than the private gain of an individual author. Historical relaciones by eyewitnesses of the American conquests could hereby serve as a sort of legal deposition or testimony in the official courtrooms of imperial policy and legislation (see Bauer 2003, 30–76).

It is in this legalistic context that Titu Cusi's critique of the conquerors' avarice and cruelty must be seen. Although it may appear as odd to the modern reader that a text addressed to the Spanish monarch engaged in what seems to be a radical indictment of the Spanish conquest, it is in fact of a piece with the scholastic political philosophy of influential voices in the Spanish

Empire, such as the Dominicans Francisco de Vitoria and Bartolomé de Las Casas, who had argued that the conquest of America was an "unjust" war by the standards of scholastic law. Their depositions were used, in turn, by the Crown to justify stripping the conquerors of their neo-feudal status by passing in 1542 the "New Laws," which revoked the conquerors' claim to an *encomienda* (a geographically defined grant of Native tribute and labor) in perpetuity. These New Laws caused outrage and defiance among the conquerors throughout the Americas and even led to the aforementioned insurrection against the Crown led by Gonzalo Pizarro. When the conquerors mobilized a legal counteroffensive, the dispute over the constitution of the Spanish Empire came to a head in a famous series of debates held in Valladolid in 1551–1552. The conquerors' legal representative, Juan Ginés de Sepúlveda, argued that the native lords of the Americas, such as the Aztecs or the Incas, had governed their subjects by way of cruelty and tyranny. Furthermore, they had engaged in violations of "natural law" (such as the Incas' habit of polygamy), all of which disqualified them from being considered legitimate rulers. Given the native lords' presumed illegitimacy as rulers, the Spanish conquest had been "just" (by scholastic legal standards) and hereby not unlike the Christians' "re-conquest" of Spain from the Moors. By implication, the Spanish conquerors of America, as participants in a "just" war, were entitled to feudal lord stature and to the tribute and labor previously claimed by the native lords. By contrast, the opposite side, represented by Las Casas, argued that the local nobles, even though previously pagans, were and continued to be the legitimate rulers of the American communities who had willingly subjected themselves to the supreme authority of the emperor Charles V and the Holy Catholic faith, not unlike the local nobility of Italy, Germany, or the Netherlands. The Spanish conquerors were therefore foreign invaders who in an "unjust" war not only perpetrated unspeakable acts of cruelty, destruction, and avarice but arrogated to themselves a status of feudal lords that rightfully belonged only to the Native nobility (see Brading, 70–71; Hanke; Pagden).

In this historical context, the apparently radical critique of Spanish abuses in Titu Cusi/Marcos García's historical narrative becomes intelligible as a politically shrewd and rhetorically persuasive exercise. The unflattering portrayal of Gonzalo Pizarro lusting after gold and Manco Inca's *coya* ("queen," although see later discussion), for example, lends specific testimony to the general arguments made by Las Casas and others about the insatiable greed, unbridled cruelty, and moral depravity of the Spanish conquerors. Similarly, the hardship and suffering imposed on the Andean communities by the Pizarro brothers' repeated attempts to extort gold and silver as ransom for captured Inca sovereigns corroborates political arguments that the unduly heavy burden in tribute and labor imposed by the conquerors on the Natives had degraded them to the status of personal slaves and was responsible for the catastrophic decimation of His Majesty's Native subjects in the Americas. Finally, the emphasis on the uncompromising loyalty of the various local leaders to Titu Cusi's father as well as on his own conversion to Christianity, reinforces the political ideal of him as a natural Christian prince *voluntarily* placing himself under the imperial protection of the king. If, admittedly, this political ideal seemed somewhat out of touch with historical reality — after all, the Vilcabamba Incas were in an official state of rebellion — the account takes pains to show that Manco Inca made the decision to remove to Vilcabamba only as a last resort, after Manco Inca's many attempts at accommodation had been frustrated and his boundless good intentions (*voluntad*) to coexist had been exhausted by Spanish treachery and greed. Titu Cusi's conversion to Christianity continues this gesture of *voluntad* for peaceful coexistence but his father's experiences and last words have understandably made him wary of the Spaniards' trustworthiness. For this reason, he requires legal assurances from the monarch that his status as the legitimate Christian prince of Peru will be respected before he can reasonably be expected to consider giving up his refuge at Vilcabamba. Thus, it is in the spirit of the (belated) realization of this political ideal—of him relinquishing his refuge and assuming his place within the Spanish imperial order—that he "relates" his version of Peruvian history to the Augustinian Marcos García, "instructs" the returning governor Lope García de Castro to present his case before the monarch, and "empowers" him to act on his behalf in all the empire's legal affairs.

As mentioned before, however, it is entirely possible that Titu Cusi's gestures of his intentions to leave Vilcabamba, including the resulting text, were but a political smokescreen created in order to delay changes to the status quo. Indeed, Spanish culture of the letter and the law constitutes only part of the context in which to read Titu Cusi's account. It would be a mistake to assume that Titu Cusi merely provided the historical "facts" while Marcos García was entirely responsible for the form of this narrative. However pervasively the form of the text was shaped by its mediations through Spanish translation and transcription, it retains distinct traces of Andean conceptions of history and conventions of historiography. In order to excavate these aspects of the text, it is helpful to place this narrative in the context of recent ethnohistorical and anthropological scholarship that has provided much insight about other histories written in Spanish but drawing on native Andean traditions. In particular, the chronicles written by Juan de Betanzos as well as those written by Pedro Cieza de León, Pedro Sarmiento de Gamboa, and during the early seventeenth century the mestizo Inca Garcilaso de la Vega contain valuable comments about Inca historiographic practices that help us to reconstruct the traditions on which Titu Cusi would have drawn when telling his history of the conquest.

Because the Incas had no alphabetic writing system, their histories were recited orally on ritual occasions as songs—sometimes described as *cantares* by Spanish observers—that were intended to celebrate the greatness of a specific ancestor and, thus, to legitimate certain claims made by his descendants. As Susan Niles has observed, these praise-narratives had narrative structures that depended heavily on mnemonic devices (xvii, 27). Such devices could include stimuli external to the narrative, such as music, war trophies especially kept for this purpose, or the Andean quipu. The quipu were strings of multicolored knotted cords arranged in particular patterns of color, texture, size, and form that encoded specific messages that could be read by persons initiated in this system, called the *quipucamayocs.* The quipu were typically used to store numerical information important for administrative purposes, such as recording tribute labor, taxes, and supplies but could also serve to assist the memories of oral historians (see Urton 1997 and 1998) (see Illustration 5). Another kind of mnemonic device was internal to the structure of the oral narrative itself, such as meter, formulaic repetition, and the performance of direct speech (Niles, 28–44). Although it is difficult to know with certainty how Titu Cusi conceived of the specific occasion when he himself performed his history before fray Marcos García, many of the events he related in his narrative were not witnessed by himself and therefore would only have been remembered by him in the form of the oral traditions about Manco Inca's life as they were being passed down by performances on such ritual occasions.

Despite the mediations through Marcos García's translation and Martín de Pando's transcription, several formal characteristics of Inca oral tradition on which Titu Cusi drew when relating his story still survive in the text. For example, narrative elements are frequently repeated ritualistically four times when they concern aspects of geography invoking the "fourness" of the Tahuantinsuyu and giving the narrative an "epic" character. The syntactical symmetry of the Spanish translation suggests that Titu Cusi's performance may have been metrical or at least followed a pat-

5. *A quipucamayoc interpreting quipus. From Guaman Poma de Ayala,* Nueva corónica y buen gobierno. *By kind permission of the Royal Library at Copenhagen (GKS 2232 4to)*

tern of rhythmical symmetry over certain passages. For purposes
of illustration we might represent such a passage here in stanza.
It relates the convergence of the various lords and their armies
from the four parts of the Tahuantinsuyu during Manco Inca's
siege of Cuzco:

> From Carmenga, which lies in the direction of the Chinchaysuyu,
> Came Coriatao, Cuillas, and Taipi, with many others
> In order to close the city's exit in that direction with their hordes.

> From the Contisuyu, which is the direction of Cachicachi,
> Came Huaman Quilcana, Curi Huallpa, all superbly equipped
>   and in battle formation,
> closing a huge gap of more than half a league wide.

> From the Collasuyu
> Came Llicllic and many other generals with a huge number of
>   men, which was in fact the largest contingent
> That formed the besieging army,

> From the Antisuyu,
> Came Antallca and Ronpa Yupanqui and many others
> in order to close the ring around the Spaniards (pp. 105–106)

> Por la parte de Carmenga, que es hacia Chinchaysuyu,
> entraron Coriatao y Cuillas y Taipi y otros muchos
> que cerraron aquel postigo con la gente que traían.

> Por la parte del Contisuyu que es hacia Cachicachi,
> entraron Huaman Quilcana y Curi Huallpa y otros muchos
> que cerraron una gran mella de más de media legua de box, todos
>   muy bien adereçados, en orden de guerra.

> Por la parte de Collasuyu
> entraron Llicllic y otros muchos capitanes con grandísima suma
>   de gente, la mayor cantidad
> que se halló en este çerco.

> Por la parte de Antisuyu
> entraron Antallca y Ronpa Yupangui y otros muchos, los quales
> acabaron de çercar el çerco que a los españoles les pusieron. (ff 167)

Similarly, certain plot elements establishing causal connections are at times rendered as a sequence of three repetitions. Thus, the plot line leading up to Manco Inca's rebellion is structured into the narration of him being taken captive and abused by the Spaniards three times. Although it is possible, of course, that this narrative sequence merely followed the actual course of historical events, I have not found any other sixteenth-century versions that present Manco Inca's decision to rebel as the result of a distinctly three-partite sequence of captivities. Most likely, this three-fold repetition is a stylistic device that was, as Niles notes, common to Inca oral traditions and that "served as a formula which facilitated the remembrance of the narratives" (40).

The narration of each of Manco Inca's captivities culminates with him giving a speech. His speeches, as well as all the other speeches that appear in the text, are never summarized or reported indirectly but always represented as direct speech. This also was, as Niles notes, a formal feature typical of Inca oral tradition, as the Inca language had no way of indicating indirect discourse (32–37). A particularly frequent convention in Inca praise narratives was hereby the representation of deathbed orations that concluded the life history of a particular Inca. Titu Cusi's narrative about his father also follows this convention. He presents not one but two deathbed orations, supposedly delivered after Manco Inca was mortally stabbed by his Spanish guests—one addressed to his subjects and one addressed specifically to his son Titu Cusi (Saire Topa is not mentioned here). Each appears as a separate chapter in the narrative with a distinct header. The highly stylized form in which he represents Manco Inca's deathbed orations points toward the performative aspects of the oral traditions from which Titu Cusi drew.

The hybrid character of this text as a history is manifest not only in its form, however, but also in its content. As exasperated modern historians have lamented when dealing with the subject of pre-Conquest Inca history generally, the colonial sources that were written based on Inca oral traditions are notoriously at odds with one another. One difficulty has been that the Inca traditions did not give dates for historical events or lifetimes of rulers, partially because their concept of history was cyclical (see MacCormack 1988). The result is that there is little consensus among modern historians about the facts and chronology of pre-Columbian Inca history. For example, although modern historians traditionally accepted a scheme developed in 1944 by John Rowe that subscribed to the idea of a chronological succession of eleven rulers beginning with the legendary founder of the dynasty Manco Capac and ended with Huayna Capac, the historicity of even this basic temporal sequence has been disputed.[24] By standards of modern European epistemologies, which emerged not coincidentally during the sixteenth century in the context of the conquest of America, historiography must aspire to an "objective" truth by attempting to "get beyond" the individual text to the historical "facts" through cross-documentary corroboration (see Cañizares-Esguerra). By these standards, the chronology and substance of most oral narrations of Inca history are problematic, and Titu Cusi's historical narrative is no exception here. Thus, the "facts" he mentions are frequently uncorroborated — even contradicted — by other surviving sixteenth-century sources.[25] For example, Titu Cusi's claim that his father Manco Inca became ruler by the explicit will of his father, Huayna Capac, and that Atahuallpa merely governed the empire until Manco Inca was old enough to assume the royal tassel is contradicted by virtually every other contemporary source and is, overall, highly unlikely to be factual (see later discussion). Even less plausible here is his claim that his father, Manco Inca, ruled Cuzco at the time when the Spaniards arrived in Peru (modern historians generally agree that Huascar ruled Cuzco before he was defeated and captured by Quisquis, who thereafter ruled Cuzco on behalf of his lord Atahuallpa). Finally, Titu Cusi's claim that he was "the one legitimate son . . . among the many sons whom my father Manco Inca Yupanqui left behind" (p. 58–59) and that his dying father had explicitly determined him as his successor is disputed by modern historians, who generally agree that after Manco Inca's death the royal tassel went to his brother Saire Topa. In fact, several contemporary chroniclers, such as the Spaniard Pedro Sarmiento de Gamboa, whose chronicle was almost contemporary with the creation of Titu Cusi's text, claimed that Titu Cusi was "not a legitimate son of Manco Inca" at all but rather a "bastard and apostate."[26] Even some of the mestizo and "Indian" chroniclers apparently were not persuaded by Titu Cusi's claim to legitimacy. Thus, he is not mentioned at all by the Inca Garcilaso de la Vega, a mestizo who wrote during the early seventeenth century; nor is he portrayed in Guaman Poma de Ayala's *Nueva corónica y buen gobierno*, also composed during the early seventeenth century, which portrays every other Inca ruler, including Manco Inca (see Illustration 6). As Luis Millones has noted,[27] Titu Cusi's account may thus have in part been produced precisely in order to affirm what he could not assume: that he was legitimate among the Inca nobility as supreme ruler. Other critics agree, identifying at least three interrelated objectives that Titu Cusi's account was meant to serve: (a) to establish his father's authority and legitimacy as Inca, despite the confusions of the pre-Conquest civil war and of the Conquest; (b) to establish the legitimacy of his own claim to the Inca throne; and (c) to expose the Spanish conquerors' claim to lordship over Peru as illegitimate (Chang Rodríguez 1980, 88). Thus, it is possibly in this light that Titu Cusi begins his history of the Conquest by giving a rationale for his legitimacy as a natural ruler: "I am the one legitimate son, meaning the eldest and first-born" (p. 58–59).

We will return to both Titu Cusi's invocation of the concept of primogeniture and to Sarmiento de Gamboa's invocation of the notion of bastardry in regard to the question of succession in a moment. Here, some general remarks about the cultural nexus of legitimacy and historiography in the pre-Hispanic Andes are first in order. Inca understanding of genealogy was based on norms of kinship that were quite different from those of Europeans. Although millions of people lived in the Tahuantinsuyu, only about 40,000 of those people were considered to be "Inca," that is, identified as members of the ethnic group that had originated and expanded their culture from Cuzco some time during the early fifteenth century. The non-Inca subjects of this empire came from other ethnic groups who had been subjugated to Inca rule, owed tribute in labor, and were generally considered to be provincials. While the Inca rulers could be ruthless in dealing with ethnic groups who resisted their expansion or those who rebelled against their rule, they were generally liberal and diplomatic with those who submitted to their supremacy, granting local lords substantial privileges and offices in the hierarchy of imperial administration and incorporating provincial deities into their own pantheon. Frequently, Inca women were married off to local lords of such provincial groups to ensure their loyalty. The Native chronicler Guaman Poma de Ayala, for example, was the offspring of such a union. By Inca cultural norms, however, offspring such as Guaman Poma, as well as the offspring of an Inca man with a non-Inca woman, would not have been considered "legitimate" Inca nobility.

Although those defined as "Inca" thus formed a privileged nobility in the empire—frequently called *orejones* (big ears) by the Spaniards because of their enlarged ears from wearing certain jewelry—not everyone in this nobility could make a legitimate claim to supreme rulership. As Catherine Julien has pointed out, legitimacy to rule was determined by an Inca noble's closeness to the hereditary line of Manco Capac, the legendary founder of the Inca dynasty. A claim to supreme rulership was thus determined by what she calls an individual's "*capac* status" (23). Hereditary descent was reckoned in Inca culture, as in European culture, patrilineally. However, as the Incas, unlike the Europeans, practiced polygamy, each new Inca ruler established his own

6. *The newly reigning Manco Inca in his ceremonial throne in Cuzco. From* Guaman Poma de Ayala, Nueva corónica y buen gobierno. *By kind permission of the Royal Library at Copenhagen (GKS 2232 4to)*

patrilineal royal descent or kinship group, called a *panaca,* that was distinct from that of his father.[28] At a given ruler's death, the members of his panaca were responsible for preserving his mummy, memory, and reputation. Each Inca oral history tradition was therefore not a general history of the Inca dynasty or realm, as was commonly aspired to by European chroniclers in sixteenth-century imperial Spain, but rather a partisan history particular to a specific panaca. Intent on exalting different founders and different descent groups that competed with one another for prestige, Inca oral traditions could thus be at great variance with one another. As Julien points out, the purpose of Inca historiography was not only to recall past glory, but also to "locate . . . members of the Inca descent group with relation to one another and to the other residents of Cuzco" (35). It is in this light that we must also see Titu Cusi's historical narrative of the Conquest, which places his father at the center of events from the very beginning, even though most other histories are in agreement that Manco Inca, because of his young age, was a relatively insignificant figure at the time of the Spanish arrival. Titu Cusi's historical account (relación) of the conquest is cast in the mold of his father's "life history," which Julien identifies as one of the two major genres of Inca oral history (91–165). By the same token, much of what Titu Cusi tells us about himself in his instrucción to Lope García de Castro revolves around his position in relation to that of Manco Inca — the primary purpose of the other major historical genre identified by Julien, which she calls the "genealogical narrative" (49–90).

How does Titu Cusi's account as a genealogical narrative and life history aim to establish both his father's and his own legitimacy as rulers? It is interesting here to consider, first, Titu Cusi's claims about Atahuallpa and Huascar. In regard to Atahuallpa, Titu Cusi says that he was "older" than Manco Inca "but a bastard" (p. 60). Although it is not entirely clear here what he means by "bastard," he later says that neither Atahuallpa nor his half-brother Huascar were "legitimate heir[s]" because, despite being "sons of Huayna Capac," their mothers were "commoners" whereas "my father had pure royal blood" (p. 61). The argument that Atahuallpa and Huascar were illegitimate because of the birth status of their mothers is significant. As Julien points out, despite the patrilineal order of reckoning descent in Inca culture, the mother's panaca, or descent group, had an important role to play in the assessment of legitimacy for rulership. Beginning with Topa Inca, the father of Huayna Capac (and grandfather of Atahuallpa, Huascar, and Manco Inca), the Inca rulers had started (or resumed) a legendary ancient tradition (allegedly already initiated by Manco Capac) of marrying only full sisters, even though they continued to have children with other women, both Inca and non-Inca. As a result, the degree of legitimacy of a potential successor relative to his (half-) brothers came to depend not so much on the descent group of his father (which would have been a given) but rather on that of his mother. The least prestige would hereby be accorded to an Inca ruler's offspring with a non-Inca mother; further up on the scale would be his offspring with a woman who was ethnically Inca (i.e., from a line originating in Cuzco) but without a claim to having descended from the line of Manco Capac; still more prestigious would be his offspring with a woman who was a coya; finally, most prestigious would be a ruler's offspring with a woman who was both coya and his full sister. The status of coya identified a woman who could, through the line of her father, claim descent from one of the eleven rulers (and, thus, from Manco Capac). It is therefore not parallel to the European "queen," who depended either on being the wedded wife of a king or on inheriting rule from a father (Julien, 35). Thus, by "commoners" Titu Cusi most likely meant that their mothers were ethnically Inca but not coya. In other words, their sons were "illegitimate" not in the European sense — that is, offspring produced with women other than a ruler's wife — but in the Andean sense of offspring produced with women whose independent hereditary status was considered to be deficient for rulership.[29]

In light of Titu Cusi's claims about the illegitimacy of Atahuallpa and Huascar as rulers based on their mothers' hereditary identity, it is significant that he provides no specifics about Manco Inca's mother except that she was, supposedly, responsible for his "pure royal blood." Nor does he tell us anything or make any claims about his own mother, except that she was in Cuzco with him while he was in Spanish custody and that she was brought to Vilcabamba with him after both had been abducted by Manco Inca's messengers. Who was Manco Inca's mother? And who was Titu Cusi's mother?

With regard to the former, Juan de Betanzos writes that "[a]lthough he [Manco Inca] was not the son of a mother who was of the ladies of Cuzco, he was the son of an important woman from the town of Anta [Jaquijahuana] which lies three leagues of the City of Cuzo" (278). The people of Anta were Incas but they had no claim to being descendants of Manco Capac. Although Manco Inca was a son of Huayna Capac, his pedigree was by Inca standards, as Julien points out, "less than ideal" (43). Yet, his pedigree was still the best among all of the living sons of Huayna Capac. Both Atahuallpa and Huascar were dead; and his brother Paullu's mother was not Inca at all but a woman from the province of Huaylas. It is for this reason that Paullu was considered a "bastard" by Guaman Poma—based on the Andean understanding of the term (Julien, 43). Also, it is possibly for this reason that Pedro Cieza de León reports that the orejones of Cuzco reacted generally positively to Francisco Pizarro's crowning of Manco Inca, replying that "they were content, and according to the ancient custom, Manco was received as Inca, and he took the fringe" (350).

As far as Titu Cusi's mother is concerned, we don't know her identity for certain. Hemming writes that she was a wife of Manco Inca "other than his full coya" (300), meaning his sister wife. Apparently he hereby follows Sarmiento de Gamboa, who is the only sixteenth-century source I am aware of that is explicit on this question (although he, too, does not give any details beyond what's already been quoted above). Sarmiento's claims in these matters, however, must be taken with a grain of salt. He wrote in 1572 on commission of Viceroy Toledo, who had his own political agenda in trying to make a case not only that the Incas were usurping and tyrannical upstarts (and therefore not "natural lords" of Peru) but also that the last "legitimate" ruler of the dynasty had been Huascar—who had, conveniently, died on orders of his brother before ever meeting any Spaniard face-to-face. This claim implied, of course, that the Spaniards had not usurped rulership from a natural lord of Tahuantinsuyu but merely filled a void that already existed upon their arrival, hereby justifying Toledo's order to have the last Inca ruler, Topa Amaru, executed. Along these lines, Sarmiento claimed that not only Titu Cusi but also his father, Manco Inca, and his uncle, Paullu, were "bastards." All three were "the lowest of all," he wrote, "for their lineage was on the side of their mothers which is what these people look at, in a question of birth" (193). Sarmiento's statement that the "side of the mother" is what "these people look at, in a question of birth" suggests that he was well aware of women's importance in Inca succession.[30] Nevertheless, his claim that both Titu Cusi and his father, Manco Inca, were "bastards" and "illegitimate" rests on the Spanish paradigm of monogamy as the foundation for an offspring's legitimacy—an idea alien to traditional Andean concepts of kinship.

However unwarranted Sarmiento's claim of Titu Cusi's bastardry was by Andean cultural norms, Titu Cusi's silence about the hereditary identity of his mother suggests that she was probably ethnically Inca but neither a coya nor Manco Inca's full sister. We must therefore assume that Hemming's inference that she had little to contribute to Titu Cusi's claim to legitimacy is warranted (even though a status of coya would not necessarily have depended on her being either Manco Inca's sister or wife). Thus, in light of the surviving information about Titu Cusi's mother, his claim to be the legitimate ("natural") ruler (based only on his patrilineal descent) appears indeed to have been rather weak by the traditional Inca succession rules. It is in this context that we must see Titu Cusi's assertion that he was "the one legitimate son, meaning the eldest and first-born, among the many sons whom my father Manco Inca Yupanqui left behind." His claim to rule on the principle of primogeniture is based on a Spanish, not an Inca, logic of succession.

Interestingly, Titu Cusi invokes the traditional Inca logic of succession in order to establish the legitimacy of his father — who had "pure royal blood" whereas his older brothers Atahuallpa and Huascar did not because their mothers were commoners (even though Titu Cusi does not tell us who, exactly, Manco Inca's mother was); by contrast, he invokes the Spanish logic of succession (primogeniture) to establish his own legitimacy. Ironically, his invocation of the primogeniture principle to establish his legitimacy would have been less than fully persuasive to his Spanish audience, who would have judged him (and indeed did judge him) as illegitimate, based on the European notion of bastardry. By European standards, legitimacy for succession depended on the identity of a mother only insofar as she was a ruler's wedded wife, not on her independent patrilineal descent from previous rulers. Therefore, despite Titu Cusi's and Sarmiento de Gamboa's evident awareness of this cultural difference, neither one was entirely successful in the act of translation.

It is difficult to determine with certainty who is responsible for these contradictions and ambiguities in Titu Cusi's account. On the one hand, it would not have been inconceivable for Titu Cusi to change traditional Inca rules of succession in his text in order to make a case for his own legitimacy. Even though Titu Cusi stressed the rules of birth (albeit not purely the traditional Inca rules) in his narrative, the Spanish envoy Diego Rodríguez de Figueroa reported that on another occasion Titu Cusi had explained to him that birthright was not ultimately of primary importance to his claim to legitimacy as ruler and that his legitimacy was based rather on merit and pragmatics: "he was in possession and was recognised by the other Incas; they all obeyed him, and if he had not the right they would not obey him" (quoted in Hemming, 300). Indeed, previous disputes regarding succession were reportedly settled by displays of strength and valor rather than strictly birthright. Thus, the ninth ruler, Inca Yupanqui (1438–1471, according to the traditional scheme of succession) had usurped the throne from his father, Pachacuti, before the latter's death after the son had successfully defended Cuzco against the invading Chanca while the father had abandoned the capital (see Rostworowski, 22–28). Moreover, the privilege accorded to the offspring of an Inca ruler and his own sister and the implications for succession resulting from this seem to have been a rather new innovation (or renovation) in Inca culture. In other words, changes in kinship practices had happened in Inca culture relatively recently before the arrival of the Spaniards and must not, therefore, necessarily and exclusively be ascribed to European colonialism.

Yet, it is possible that Titu Cusi's pragmatist arguments were a more or less realistic reflection of the historical impact of the cataclysmic events just before and during the Conquest upon Inca logic of succession. As Julien points out (42–47), the combined impacts of the pre-Hispanic civil war in Peru (in which Huascar and scores of his descent group died), European diseases (killing both Huayna Capac and his heir), as well as Atahuallpa's murder by the Spaniards left a tremendous stress on the traditional Inca logic of succession resumed by Huayna Capac's father. This situation was further aggravated when the Spanish conquerors, in search of wives, seized on the female Inca nobility. Titu Cusi's unforgettable account of Gonzalo Pizarro's demand that he be given Manco Inca's sister-wife, Cura Oclo, as a wife and Manco

Inca's attempt to deceive Pizarro by giving him another woman, Ynguill, in her stead is a good illustration of this (see p. 96). Despite Manco Inca's ingenuity here, he ultimately failed to protect both Inca noblewomen against the Spanish suitors. As Titu Cusi relates, Cura Oclo did fall into the hands of Gonzalo Pizarro, was abused by the Spaniards, and tried to resist their advances by "covering her body with stinking and filthy things" before being murdered in Spanish custody (p. 124; also Hemming, 183). Ynguill, as Julien points out, may have been Francisca Ynguill, who became the wife of Juan Pizarro (305, n. 13). Although it appears that both of Titu Cusi's brothers, Saire Topa and Topa Amaru, had more legitimacy for rulership than he did, ultimately even the claim to legitimacy of their common father, Manco Inca, was weak by traditional logic of succession. In pre-Hispanic times, Manco Inca might have settled such a controversy as Atahuallpa (and some of his predecessors) had done—by wiping out the panaca of any competitor for succession. The Spanish invasion, however, not only changed the balance of power but also brought the introduction of alphabetic writing to Andean historiographic practices; therefore, such a "new beginning" of history became more difficult to orchestrate. Ultimately then, the fact that Titu Cusi's account appears to be particularly at odds with other surviving versions based on different panaca traditions may be explained by the dwindling power of this penultimate Inca compared to that still commanded by his grandfather, who was the last undisputed ruler to consolidate his power over the entire Tahuantinsuyu.

On the other hand, there can be no doubt that some of the ambiguities with regard to Andean and Spanish cultural concepts crept into the text only with fray Marcos García's translation. Especially some of the glosses over native Andean cultural concepts are unequivocally the marks of his interventions and impositions. One example is the account of Atahuallpa's sensitive reaction toward Vicente de Valverde's fateful presentation of the breviary as the result of the Inca's lingering annoyance with the Spaniards' disregard for his offer of a ceremonial drink. Marcos García translates Titu Cusi's Quechua account like this: "My uncle, still offended by the wasting of the *chicha* (which is how we call our drink) took the letter (or whatever it was) and threw it down" (p. 60–61). Although this passage seems to reflect upon the Inca principle of reciprocity (see Classen, 1–2, 59–60), it is noteworthy that chicha was not a Quechua word but was imported by the Spanish from the Caribbean. This suggests that fray Marcos García is falsely representing Titu Cusi's use of the first person plural ("we") here.[31] It is difficult to decide whether these misrepresentations of Andean culture result from Marcos García's imperfect grasp of Quechua or from his deliberate manipulations, possibly intended to lend his translation an air of authenticity.

Only slightly more ambiguous in regard to agency is the use of various Christian and Andean religious concepts in this text — concepts such as "God" (*Dios*), "Viracocha," "Devil" (*demonio*), and "*supai*." It is doubtful, for example, that the cultural gloss on supai — "which is to say the Devil in our language" (p. 76) — can be attributed to Titu Cusi. The word in pre-colonial Quechua simply meant "a supernatural being that could be both malignant and benevolent." Domingo Santo Tomás's 1560 dictionary still translates *çupay* as "demonio, bueno o malo" (99), thus bearing testimony to the incommensurability of Christian and Andean religious concepts by allowing for the idea of a "demonio, bueno." In pre-Christian Quechua the word appears to have meant something more value neutral, perhaps better translated as "mountain spirit."[32] In light of Titu Cusi's noted tolerance of Christianity and reluctance to give up native Andean *huacas*, its use in the Manichean sense of evil here suggests the imprint of Marcos García's monotheistic missionary jargon on this text.

A final example of ambiguous agency in this text is Titu Cusi's account of the miraculous appearance of an equestrian knight, recognizable to Spanish readers as Santiago, patron saint of Spain, in support of the Spanish siege of Cuzco. Is this a Native tradition repeated by Titu Cusi or a liberty taken by the Spanish translator or the mestizo scribe?[33] It is difficult to decide for this early text, but it is worth mentioning that by the early seventeenth century this story apparently had become part of native Andean memories, for it was repeated and illustrated by Guaman Poma de Ayala (see Illustration 7). To be sure, Guaman Poma's version must also be taken with a grain of salt, because he was not, as mentioned above, considered to be a member of the Inca nobility (being connected to it only through his mother's lineage) and tended to portray Inca religion from the perspective of a Christian convert (even though he praised the civic accomplishments of the Inca state). In any case, Marcos García's translation of Titu Cusi's oral version of this story might well present an early manifestation of the hybridization of various European and Andean traditions of the history of the Conquest from which Guaman Poma could draw roughly half a century later.

Regarding the hybridity of Titu Cusi's account of the conquest of Tahuantinsuyu, a final word is in order also about Martín de Pando, Titu Cusi's mestizo secretary who transcribed Marcos García's Spanish dictation into manuscript form. He had arrived, along with Juan de Betanzos, at Vilcabamba in 1560 as part of an embassy sent by the corregidor (royal administrator) of Cuzco, Juan Polo de Ondegardo, in order to assure the Vilcabamba rebels that the deceased Saire Topa had died a natural death. After the embassy's mission had been completed, Titu Cusi, aware of the advantages of having a person knowledgeable of European culture at Vilcabamba, persuaded the mestizo to stay. Pando accepted the invitation, serving Titu Cusi as secretary, confidant, and advisor for the rest of his life. Titu Cusi seems to have appreciated his company a great deal, frequently practicing European-style fencing with him and using Pando's writing skills in his correspondence with Spanish authorities. Because Pando stayed,

7. *St. James the Great, Apostle of Christ, intervenes in the war for Cuzco. From* Guaman Poma de Ayala, Nueva corónica y buen gobierno. *By kind permission of the Royal Library at Copenhagen (GKS 2232 4to)*

continuously as far as we can tell, at Vilcabamba from 1560 until his death in 1571, it is uncertain whether he would have seen a copy of either the first bilingual Spanish/Quechua dictionary or the first grammar of the Quechua language, both of which had been completed by the Dominican clergyman Domingo de Santo Tomás in Peru and printed in Valladolid by the royal printer Francisco Fernández de Cordoba in 1560 (see Illustration 8). A comparison of Pando's transcriptions of Quechua words and Santo Tomás's dictionary is inconclusive as to the question of whether he transcribed Quechua words simply as they seemed to him grapho-phonemically most accurate or whether he consulted Santo Tomás's first attempt at a standardized orthography of the Quechua language in European alphabet. The evidence suggesting the former seems to preponderate. Some of his transcriptions basically correspond with Santo Tomás's dictionary, such as *yllapa*, *Viracocha*, and *macho*, but others do not, such as his transcription of *supai* (p. 76) compared to Santo Tomás's *çupay* (*Lexicon*, 279). Also, Pando's orthography is not always internally consistent—which at the least suggests that Pando was not consistently using Santo Tomás's works during the transcription process even if he owned or had seen copies. For example, he spells the plural form of the Quechua word for "knife" as *tomës* in one place but *tumës* in another (see p. 61 and p. 62). Similarly inconsistent are his renderings of grammatical forms, such as the plural of Quechua nouns. Some of these forms follow Spanish, not Quechua, rules. For example, the manuscript represents the plural of *yllapa* (thunderclap) as *yllapas*. At other times, however, Pando transcribes forms that appear to be Hispanized spellings following Quechua grammatical forms, such as *Apocona* (Lords; *Apu* means "lord" and the suffix *-kuna* signifies the plural form, but rendered *Appó* and *-cona* by Santo Tomás's *Lexicon* and *Gramática*). However, these Quechua plural forms are inconsistent in the manuscript and, at times, hybridized with Spanish plural forms; for instance, in Pando's transcription *yanaconas* (p.

121) (*yana-cona-s: yana* means "dedicated servant" and the suffix *-kuna* [or *-cona*] signifies plural in Quechua but *-s* is apparently derived from Castilian vernacular grammar). A full-scale analysis of these hybridized linguistic forms is not appropriate here. A future first step in this direction may lie in definitively establishing which forms can plausibly be ascribed to Pando and which ones to Marcos García. Those attributable to the mestizo Martín de Pando may well point toward the heteroglossia pervading the still unstandardized pigeon culture of which he was born, a culture in which Old World and New World linguae francae and vernaculars mixed, fused, and hybridized to make new standards in future generations.

A Note on Quechua Terms and Orthography

Regarding the translation of indigenous concepts and orthography in the present introduction and edition, I have chosen to use a European concept throughout in order to convey an Andean concept in cases where a European concept is semantically broad enough. For example, when I use the term "Inca Empire" interchangeably with "Tahuantinsuyu," I do so in the broadest sense of "empire" as a polity that territorially expanded beyond its original ethnic boundaries, recognizing the important differences between the Andean geographically expansive polity and what Europeans would associate with the term "empire." In other cases, I have used European concepts provisionally and in quotation marks until an explanation of the Andean concept was in order. An example of this would be the European concept of "queen" and the (not identical) Andean concept of coya. As far as my orthographic rendering of Andean names that commonly occur in historical and literary scholarship, I have, after some wavering, finally chosen to go with the Hispanized version rather than the grapho-phonemically more precise spelling representing the velar/postvelar contrasts that was standardized by the Peruvian

LEXICON, O

Vocabulario de la lengua general
del PERV, cõpuefto por el Maeftro
F.Domingo de.S.Thomas de la orden
de.S.Domingo.

S.Dominicus Prædicatorum dux.

Impreffo en Valladolid, por Francifco Fernan-
dez de Cordoua, Impreffor de la. M.R.
CON PRIVILEGIO.

8. *Frontispiece of Domingo Santo Tomás's* Lexicon o Vocabulario *(1560).*
Library of Congress, Rare Book Room

Ministry of Education during the 1970s and since has been used in some recent anthropological and historical scholarship (see, for example, D'Altroy). This decision was made purely on pragmatic grounds, as most of the scholars cited in this introduction still used Hispanized orthography and, therefore, it would have been unnecessarily confusing and complicated to represent two systems of spelling in this Introduction or to change the spellings of my modern secondary sources.

For the same reason, I have used Hispanized orthography in the translation of the text when rendering common Quechua names and words that have already been solidified in modern scholarship. Thus, I write "Inca" rather than "Inka," "Atahuallpa" rather than "Atawallpa," "Huascar" rather than "Wasqar," "huacas" rather than "wakas," "coya" rather than "qoya," and so on. In my rendering of Quechua words that do not commonly occur in modern scholarship (such as *tomëe*), however, I attempt to decipher the original manuscript rather than previous Spanish editions. In these cases, I also note Santo Tomás's first "standardized" sixteenth-century orthography as well as modern (meaning post-1970s) official orthography, citing the *Diccionario Quechua-Español-Quechua* by the Academia Mayor de la lengua Quechua and Laura Ladrón de Guevara Cuadro's *Diccionario Quechua-Ingles-Español. Español-Quechua-Ingles. Quechua-Ingles-Español.* In references to primary and secondary sources, I have used English translations when adequate ones were available.

The Manuscript and Previous Editions

The manuscript of Titu Cusi Yupanqui's *Instrucción* is today preserved in the Biblioteca del Monasterio de San Lorenzo del Escorial. Some time after its arrival there, it was bound as one section in a volume of several manuscripts and subtitled "De las relaciones del tiempo de la visita. Relación del gobierno y sucesión de los Ingas." Its pages were apparently numbered by the person who bound it, for its first page corresponds to page 130 in that volume. In my page references to the manuscript, I cite the pagination applied in this volume.

The text has been published in numerous Spanish editions during the twentieth century in the wake of growing interest in Amerindian perspectives on the European conquest of America. In some respects it shares a common editorial history with other texts by colonial Latin American Indians, such as Felipe Guaman Poma de Ayala (1615) or Juan de Santacruz Pachacuti Yamqui (1613) (see Bauer 2001). Like Guaman Poma's *Nueva corónica y buen gobierno,* it was forgotten for more than three centuries. Parts of the text were first published in 1877 by Marcos Jiménez de la Espada as an appendix to his edition of Pedro Cieza de León's *Guerra de Quito.* A first complete edition was published in Lima in 1916 under the title *Relación de la conquista del Perú y hechos del Inca Manco II* by Horacio H. Urteaga with a biography of Titu Cusi by Carlos Romero. Urteaga's transcription was republished in Lima with a new introduction and notes by Francisco Carillo in 1973. In 1985 Luis Millones published in Lima a new transcription that retained — more closely than Urteaga's — the orthographic particularities of the original and indicated the page breaks of the manuscript. Similarly, Liliana Regalado de Hurtado's 1992 edition with a new transcription retained the orthographic characteristics of the manuscript and added a glossary of Quechua terms appearing in the text, as well as onomastic and toponymic indexes. In 1988 María del Carmen Martín Rubio published the first (peninsular) Spanish edition of the text, and in 2001 Alessandra Luiselli published the first Mexican edition, which substantially normalized and modernized the sixteenth-century orthography for the modern reader. There have also been several translations into other languages of Titu Cusi's *Instrucción.* Hidefuji Someda prepared a Japanese translation, Martin Lienhard a German translation, and John H. Parry and Robert Keith translated some short excerpts into English in their collection titled *New Iberian World* (1984).

In preparing this full-length English translation, I have consulted the extant published editions as well as the original manuscript. I was able to inspect the manuscript at the Royal Library of the Escorial in winter 2002–2003 and also to obtain a photocopy of the microfilm copy housed at the Library of the Royal Palace in Madrid by kind permission and assistance of the library staff there. As the manuscript is at times difficult to decipher, it is not surprising to find occasional discrepancies among the existing Spanish transcriptions of the text, which I duly note. In my translation, I have made an effort to strike a balance between remaining as close to the original as possible while rendering it in idiomatic English. I have preserved the paragraph breaks (which are indicated in the manuscript as lines drawn from the last word of a line to the margin) but have frequently broken up long sentences, more common in Spanish than in English, into smaller syntactic units. Although perhaps not always successful, I have taken pains to find current English idioms to capture the sense of the Spanish original as closely as possible. It is my hope in presenting this translation to the public that it will be found useful for scholars, teachers, and students of colonial (Latin) American and Native American history, culture, and literature.

Notes

1. Since completing the manuscript, it has come to my attention that Catherine Julien has also completed a full-length translation of Titu Cusi's text, which is forthcoming. The two translations have evolved independently from on another, and I would like to thank Catherine Julien for bringing her forthcoming translation to my attention.

2. On Inca expansionism, see María Rostworowski de Diez Canseco, *History of the Inca Realm*, trans. Harry B. Iceland (Cambridge: Cambridge University Press, 1999), 12–134; also Terence D'Altroy, *The Incas* (Malden, MA, and Oxford, England: Blackwell Publishers, 2002), 109–262; John Murra, *El Mundo Andino: población, medio ambiente y economía* (Lima:

Pontifica Universidad Católica del Perú, 2002), 41–82; and Kenneth Andrien, *Andean Worlds: Indigenous History, Culture, and Consciousness under Spanish Rule, 1532–1825* (Albuquerque: University of New Mexico Press, 2001), 14–39. On the circumstances of Huayna Capac's death, see Michael Moseley, *The Incas and Their Ancestors* (London: Thames and Hudson, 1992), 7–11.

3. Titu Cusi reports that they "digen que vienen por el viento." Titu Cusi Yupanqui's *Ynstrucción del Ynga Diego de Castro Titu Cussi Yupanqui* (In "De las relaciones del tiempo de la visita. Relación del gobierno y sucesión de los Ingas," Biblioteca del Real Monasterio de San Lorenzo de El Escorial, Manuscrito L. I. 5, folio 141 (64).

4. On the background of Pizarro and the other men in his band, see James Lockhart, *The Men of Cajamarca: Social and Biographical Study of the First Conquerors of Peru* (Austin: University of Texas Press, 1972), especially 135–156; also Rafael Varón Gabai, *Francisco Pizarro and His Brothers: The Illusion of Power in Sixteenth-century Peru*, Trans. Javier Flores Espinoza (Norman: University of Oklahoma Press, 1997), 3–35.

5. For more details on this struggle for the royal tassel, see Rostworowski, *History of the Inca Realm*, 110–134; also John Hemming, *The Conquest of the Incas* (New York: Harcourt Brace Jovanovich, 1970), 28–35.

6. For a more detailed account of these events, see Hemming, *The Conquest of the Incas*, 23–70; also Karen Spalding, *Huarochirí, An Andean Society under Inca and Spanish Rule* (Stanford: Stanford University Press, 1984), 106–135.

7. For a discussion of these complex Hispano-Andean alliances that were instrumental in the Spanish conquest, see Steve Stern, *Peru's Indian Peoples and the Challenge of Spanish Conquest: Huamanga to 1640* (Madison: University of Wisconsin Press, 1993); also Waldemar Espinoza Soriano, *Destrucción del imperio de los incas: la rivalidad política y señorial de los curacazgos andinos* (Lima, Ediciones Retablo de Papel, 1973).

8. See Hemming, *The Conquest of the Incas*, 89–229; also Andrien, *Andean Worlds*, 41–43.

9. For a detailed account of the neo-Inca state, see Hemming, *The Conquest of the Incas*, 256–346; also George Kubler, "The Neo-Inca State (1537–1572)," *The Hispanic American Historical Review* 27:2 (1947): 189–200.

10. For more detailed accounts of the civil wars, see James Lockhart, *Spanish Peru, 1532–1560* (Madison: University of Wisconsin Press, 1994), 137–140; also Andrien, *Andean Worlds,* 43–49; and Hemming, *The Conquest of the Incas,* 227–272.

11. Edmundo Guillén Guillén (*Versión inca de la conquista* [Lima: Editorial Milla Batres, 1974], 11), has surmised that Saire Topa was poisoned; however, the circumstances of his death have not been definitively established.

12. For a good recent account of Juan Santos Atahuallpa's rebellion, see Hanne Veber, "Ashánika Messianism," *Current Anthropology* 44:2 (April 2003): 183–211; on Andean resistance more generally, see Andrien, *Andean Worlds,* 193–232.

13. For a more comprehensive discussion of Native appropriations of European sign systems for the purpose of resistance, see Raquel Chang-Rodríguez, *La apropiación del signo: Tres cronistas indígenas del Perú* (Tempe: Center for Latin American Studies, Arizona State University, 1988), and ibid., "Writing as Resistance: Peruvian History and the Relación of Titu Cussi Yupanqui," in R. Adorno, ed., *From Oral to Written Expression.* For a more general account of Incan versions of the conquest, see Guillén Guillén, *Versión inca de la conquista,* and ibid., "Titu Cussi Yupanqui y su tiempo, El estado imperial inca y su trágico final: 1572." *Historia y Cultura* no. 13–14 (Lima: Museo Nacional de Historia, 1981): 61–99.

14. Although southern Peruvian Quechua had served as the administrative lingua franca of Tahuantinsuyu, the Incas had never enforced linguistic standardization or uniformity. As a result, the Spaniards upon their arrival in Peru found a bewildering linguistic diversity—José de Acosta claims that there were more than 700 languages in the Inca realm (see Andrien, *Andean Worlds,* 117)—and promoted a standardized version of southern Peruvian Quechua as a *lengua general* (lingua franca) for the purpose of catechization and instruction (see Sabine Dedenbach-Salazar and Lindsey Crickmay, eds. *La lengua de la cristianización en Latinoamérica: Catequización e instrucción en lenguas amerindias/The Language of Christianization in Latin America: Catechisation and Instruction in Amerindian Languages* [Markt Schwaben: Saurwein, 1999]).

15. For historical accounts of this movement, see Stern, *Peru's Indian Peoples,* 50–55; Sabine MacCormack, *Religion in the Andes: Vision and*

Imagination in Early Colonial Peru (Princeton, NJ: Princeton University Press, 1991), 175–81; and Andrien, *Andean Worlds,* 168–171.

16. For an account of Ortiz's martyrdom, see also the account given by Doña Angelina Llacsa, one of the Inca's wives, published as an appendix to Urteaga's edition of Titu Cusi's account (*Relación de la Conquista del Perú y hechos del Inca Manco II,* ed. Horacio H. Urteaga, Collección de Libros y Documentos relativos a la Historia del Perú, t. II [Lima: Imprenta y Librería San Martí y Compañía, 1916], 133–137.

17. This is the interpretation that John Hemming gives of these continuous overtures of goodwill that remained, however, without concrete result for the Spaniards (Hemming, *Conquest of the Incas,* 338–339).

18. The Inca Garcilaso de la Vega, writing in the early seventeenth century, claimed that the land and labor granted to Saire Topa in exchange for his return to Cuzco—a grant that included substantial parts of Huayna Capac's estate and that Titu Cusi's son stood to inherit in a marriage to Beatriz—had already been divided up among the Spanish citizens of Cuzco at the time the grant was made. For more on the fate of Huayna Capac's estate, see Susan Niles, *The Shape of Inca History: Narrative and Architecture in an Andean Empire* (Iowa City: University of Iowa Press, 1999), 121–153.

19. For a discussion of the Andean oral traditions surrounding this scene, see Regina Harrison, *Signs, Songs, and Memory in the Andes: Translating Quechua Language and Culture* (Austin: University of Texas Press, 1989); also Jesús Lara, *La poesía quechua* (Mexico City: Fondo de Cultura Económica, 1979), 92; and Nathan Wachtel, *The Vision of the Vanquished: The Spanish Conquest of Peru through Indian Eyes, 1530–1570,* trans. Ben and Siân Reynolds (New York: Barnes and Noble, 1977), 35. On Andean oral traditions more generally see also Margot Beyersdorff, and Sabine Dedenbach-Salazar Sáenz, eds., *Andean Oral Traditions: Discourse and Literature/Tradiciones Orales Andinas: Discurso y Literatura* (Bonn: Bonner Amerikanistische Studien, 1994).

20. Because of the multiple and culturally diverse agencies involved in the production of this text, Alessandra Luiselli has written of the "mestizo discursivity" of Titu Cusi's text ("Introducción," in *Instrucción del Inca don Diego de Castro Titu Cusi Yupanqui,* ed. Alessandra Luiselli [Mexico: Universidad Nacional Autónoma de México, 2001], 17); on

the question of translation, see also Gustavo Verdesio, "Traducción y contrato en la obra de Titu Cusi Yupanqui," *Bulletin of Hispanic Studies* LXXII (1995): 403–412.

21. Andrien, *Andean Worlds*, 106. On cultural contact and conflict in colonial Peru, see also Susan Elizabeth Ramírez, *The World Upside Down: Cross-Cultural Contact and Conflict in Sixteenth-Century Peru* (Stanford: Stanford University Press, 1996).

22. See Roberto González Echevarría, "Humanismo, Retórica y las Crónicas de la Conquista," in *Isla a su Vuelo Fugitiva. Ensayos Críticos sobre Literatura Hispanoamericana* (Madrid: José Porrúa Turanzas, S. A. 1983), 9–26; also ibid., *Myth and Archive: A Theory of Latin American Narrative* (Cambridge: Cambridge University Press, 1990).

23. Walter Mignolo, "El Métatexto Historiográfico y la Historiografía Indiana," *MLN* 96:2 (1981): 389; see also ibid., "Cartas, crónicas y relaciones del descubrimiento y la conquista, in *Historia de la literatura hispanoamericana; época colonial,* ed. Luis Iñigo Madrigal (Madrid: Ediciones Cátedra, 1982), 57–116.

24. For a discussion of this controversy, see Catherine Julien, *Reading Inca History* (Iowa City: University of Iowa Press, 2000), 6–9.

25. See Guillermo Lohmann Villena, "El Inka Titu Cusi Yupanqui y su entrevista con el oidor Matienzo (1565)" *Mercurio Peruano* 66 (1941): 4.

26. Pedro Sarmiento de Gamboa, "History of the Incas," in Sir Clements Markham, ed., *History of the Incas by Sarmiento de Gamboa and The Execution of the Inca Tupac Amaru by Captain Baltasar de Ocampo, trans. and ed. by Sir Clements Markham* (London: Hakluyt Society, 1907), 193. This is repeated during the early seventeenth century by Baltasar de Ocampo, who wrote that Titu Cusi was not "the natural and legitimate Lord of that land (he being a bastard) having no right" (Ocampo, 213).

27. See Luis Millones, "Introducción," *Ynstrucción del Ynga Don Diego de Castro Titu Cusi Yupangui,* edición facsímil de Luis Millones (Lima, Ediciones El Virrey, 1985), 7. For an extended discussion of these historical inaccuracies, see Carlos Romero, "Biografía de Tito Cusi Yupanqui," in Diego de Castro Titu Cusi Yupanqui, *Relación de la Conquista del Perú y hechos del Inca Manco II,* ed. Horacio H. Urteaga, Collección de Libros y Documentos relativos a la Historia del Perú, t. II (Lima: Imprenta y Librería San Martí y Compañía, 1916), xxii–xxiv.

28. For a more detailed discussion of this kinship logic, see D'Altroy, *Incas,* 89–103; Niles, *Shape of Inca History,* 1–27; also Julien, *Reading Inca History,* 23–48.

29. Not surprisingly, Titu Cusi's claim that Atahuallpa's and Huascar's mothers were commoners is contradicted by chronicles that drew from other oral traditions. Thus, Betanzos, whose wife, Angelina Yupanqui, had formerly been Atahuallpa's sister-wife, claimed that Atahuallpa's mother was Pallacoca, a "noble lady of Cuzco" of the "lineage of Inca Yupanque" and thus a descendant of Manco Capac (Juan de Betanzos, *Narrative of the Incas,* trans. and ed. by Roland Hamilton and Dana Buchanan from the Palma de Mallorca manuscript [Austin: University of Texas Press, 1996], 178). Sarmiento de Gamboa, however, claimed that Atahuallpa's mother was Tocto Coca, who was Huayna Capac's "cousin" and "of the lineage of Inca Yupanqui" ("History of the Incas," 169). Although Betanzos makes a claim for Atahuallpa's legitimacy, Sarmiento calls Atahuallpa "illegitimate" because Huascar was the son of Araua Ocllo, Huayna Capac's "sister" (160).

30. Generally, Europeans often did not understand the difference between the European concept of *queen* and the Andean concept of coya. Domingo de Santo Tomás's dictionary, for example, defines coya as *"reyna, o emperatriz, muger de emperador o de rey"* (*Lexicon o vocabulario de la lengua general del Peru* [1560], edición facsimilar por Raúl Porras Barrenechea [Lima: Edición del instituto de Historia, 1951], 266). A woman's status as *coya,* however, depended not on her being the "wife" or a ruler but rather, as pointed out above, on her claim to descent from Manco Capac by her paternal line.

31. I am obliged to the anonymous reader for the University of Colorado Press for this observation.

32. On the meaning of this word in Quechua, see Pierre Duviols, "Camaquen, Upani: un concept animiste des anciens peruviens," Amerikanistische Studien I, Festschrift für Hermann Trimborn anlässlich seines 75, Geburtstages = Estudios americanistas I, Libro jubilar en homenaje a Hermann Trimborn con motivo de su septuagésimo-quinto aniversario / Hartmann, Roswith, éd; Oberem, Udo, Éd (Collectanea instituti Anthropos, 20) (St. Augustin: Haus Völker und Kultures, Anthropos-Institut, 1978), 132–144; also ibid., "La destrucción de las

religiones andinas: conquista y colonia." *Historia general*, 9 (México: Universidad nacional autónoma de México. UNAM, Instituto de investigaciones históricas), 441–459. On the changes in Andean religious concepts resulting from European conquest and colonialism more general, see also Arthur Demarest, *Viracocha: The Nature and Antiquity of the Andean High God* (Cambridge, MA, Peabody Museum of Archaeology and Ethnology, Harvard University, 1991); Willem F.H. Adeelar, "A grammatical category for manifestations of the supernatural in early colonial Quechua," in *Language in the Andes*, ed. Peter Cole, Gabriella Hermon, and Mario Daniel Martín (Newark: University of Delaware, 1994), 116–125; and Sabine Dedenbach-Salazar, "La terminología cristiana en textos quechuas de instrucción religiosa en el siglo XVI, in *Latin American Indian Literatures: Messages and Meanings,* ed. Mary Preuss (Lancaster, CA: Labyrinthos, 1997), 195–209; and ibid., ". . . luego no puedes negar que ay Dios Criador del mundo, pues tus Incas con no ser Christianos lo alcanzaron a sauer, y lo llamaron Pachacamac," La lengua de la cristianización en los Sermones de los misterios de nuestra santa fe catolica de Fernando de Avendaño (1649), in *La lengua de la cristianización en Latinoamérica: Catequización e instrucción en lenguas amerindias/The Language of Christianization in Latin America: Catechisation and Instruction in Amerindian Languages,* Sabine Dedenbach-Salazar and Lindsey Crickmay, eds. (Markt Schwaben: Saurwein, 1999), 223–248.

33. Luiselli ("Introducción," 82, n. 39) suggests that this may have to be attributed to Marcos García.

Translation of Titu Cusi Yupanqui's Account

The Inca Don Diego de Castro Titu Cusi Yupanqui's Instruction to the very illustrious Señor licentiate Lope García de Castro, formerly Governor of this kingdom of Peru, concerning the affairs in which the latter is authorized by power of attorney to negotiate with His Majesty on the former's behalf.

As I, Diego de Castro Titu Cusi Yupanqui, grandson of Huayna Capac[1] and son of Manco Inca Yupanqui,[2] the natural lords that used to rule these kingdoms and provinces of Peru, have received many graces and favors from the very illustrious Señor licentiate Lope García de Castro, formerly governor of these kingdoms by the grace of His Majesty, King Don Philip, our lord; and as Your

Excellency are a person of great valor and piety who are about to leave these kingdoms for those of Spain, it seems to me that I couldn't have a person with better credentials and disposition to serve as an advocate on my behalf before His Majesty regarding certain affairs of utmost importance to me and my sons and descendants. As I put great confidence in Your Excellency, I do not hesitate to entrust all my affairs to your hands. Furthermore, as Your Excellency has always shown me such great favors in all things, I hope that I may find your support also in this very important matter.

As the memory of men is frail and weak, it would be impossible to remember everything accurately with regard to all our great and important affairs unless we avail ourselves of writing to assist us in our purposes. Therefore, it is necessary for me, being as brief as possible, to call to mind a few important issues. I hope that Your Excellency may favor me by bringing these concerns, which I will momentarily detail, to the attention of His Majesty on my behalf. These are the following.

First, that Your Excellency, upon your safe arrival in Spain, may do me the favor of enlightening His Majesty the King, our lord Don Philip under whose protection I have placed myself, about my identity and the hardships I suffer in these jungles as a result of His Majesty's and His vassals' having taken possession of this land, which belonged to my ancestors. Perhaps His Excellency could begin by giving a testimony about who and whose son I am, so that His Majesty is entirely clear on the reasons why I am entitled to compensation.

I suppose that it is common knowledge by now, given the accounts of many people, who the ancient and legitimate lords of this country were, from where and under what circumstances they came; therefore, there is no need to be detained by explanations. But I would greatly appreciate it if Your Excellency could do me the honor of informing His Majesty that I am the one legitimate son, meaning the eldest and firstborn, among the many sons whom my father Manco Inca Yupanqui left behind.[3] He entrusted me to take care of them and to look after them as I would of myself. This is what I have been doing from the day he died up to this very day; and this is what I am doing now and what I will continue to do as long as God keeps me alive, because it is right that sons do what their fathers have ordered them to do, especially during their last days. His Majesty should also be informed that my father, Manco Inca Yupanqui, as the son of Huayna Capac and grandson of Topa Inca Yupanqui,[4] and thus the descendant of their ancestors in a direct line, was the highest ruler of all these kingdoms of Peru. As such, he was designated by his father Huayna Capac and, after the latter's death, recognized and respected by everyone throughout the land, as I, too, was then, am now, and have been ever since my father's death.[5] Furthermore, I would be much obliged if Your Excellency could explain to His Majesty the reasons why I am now in such dire straits in these jungles where my father left me after the Spaniards ruined and then murdered him.

Moreover, His Majesty should be made aware of the things that are explained in more detail below with regard to the manner and times in which the Spaniards intruded into these lands of Peru and of the way they treated my father while he was still alive before they killed him in this land, which is now mine. The account is as follows.

The Account of how the Spaniards intruded into Peru and of the Things that Manco Inca did when he lived among them

At the time when the Spaniards first landed in this country of Peru and when they arrived at the city of Cajamarca, which is about 190 leagues from here,[6] my father Manco Inca was residing in the city of Cuzco. There he governed with all the powers that had been bestowed upon him by his father Huayna Capac.[7]

He first learned of the Spaniards' arrival from certain messengers who had been sent from there by one of his brothers by the name of Atahuallpa, who was older but a bastard,[8] and by some Indians from the lowlands called Tallanas, who live on the coast of the South Sea, fifteen or twenty leagues from Cajamarca. They reported having observed that certain people had arrived in their land, people who were very different from us in custom and dress, and that they appeared to be Viracochas (this is the name that we used to apply to the creator of all things, calling him *Teqsi Viracocha*, which means "origin" and "originator of all things").[9] They named the people as such because they differed much from us in clothing and appearance and because they rode very large animals with silver feet (by which they meant the glittering horseshoes). Another reason for calling them so was that the Indians saw them alone talking to white cloths [paños blancos] as a person would speak to another, which is how the Indians perceived the reading of books and letters. Moreover, they called them Viracochas because of the stately appearance of their persons and because each was so different from the other, some having black beards and others red ones and, finally, because they saw them eat out of silver dishes und using *yllapas*,[10] which is the word we use for "thunder" and by which they meant their "guns"; for they thought that the thunder they made came from the sky.

Two of these Viracochas were brought to my uncle Atahuallpa by some men from the Yunca people. At the time, Atahuallpa was staying at Cajamarca, where he received them very well. However, when he offered our customary drink in a golden cup to one of them, the Spaniard poured it out with his own hands, which offended my uncle very much. After that, those two Spaniards showed my uncle a letter or a book (I am not sure exactly which), explaining to him that this was the *quillca* [word] of God and of the king. My uncle, still offended by the wasting of the *chicha* (which is how we call our drink),[11] took the letter (or whatever it was) and threw it down, saying, "What is this supposed to be that you gave to me here? Be gone!" Thereupon the Spaniards returned to their companions and related to them what they had seen and what had happened during their dealings with my uncle Atahuallpa.[12]

Many days later, my uncle Atahuallpa was engaged in war and altercations with one of his brothers, Huascar Inca, over the question of who was the rightful king of this land. In truth, neither one of them was the legitimate heir, for they had only usurped the power from my father, who was still a boy then. However, each of them made claims based on various uncles and relatives and argued that, although their father may have named my father king in his last days, a boy could not be king and that, therefore, it would be better if one of the elder ones, not the child, be king. Of course, these justifications were hardly motivated by sound reason but rather by passions of greed and ambition; for, although both were sons of Huayna Capac, their mothers were commoners, whereas my father had pure royal blood, as had Pachacuti Inca, the grandfather of Huayna Capac.[13] In any case, while these two brothers—sons of different mothers—were caught up in these said altercations, it was reported that forty or fifty Spaniards had arrived at Cajamarca, the town mentioned above, on their well-equipped horses. My uncle Atahuallpa learned of this while he was celebrating a certain festival in a town called Guamachuco, which is not far from there, and immediately set out with his entourage. However, he brought no weapons for battle or harnesses for defense, only *tomës* (which is how we call our knives) and *lassos* for the purpose of hunting this new kind of llamas,[14] which is how we called our livestock and also their horses, since we had never seen any before). Not concerned about the few people who had come or interested in who they were, they brought only the tomës and knives for skinning and quartering the animals.

When my uncle was approaching Cajamarca with all of his people, the Spaniards met them at the springs of Conoc, one and a half leagues from Cajamarca. Having arrived there, he asked them why they had come, and they answered that they had come on orders of Viracocha in order to tell them how to get to know him. After having heard what they had to say, my uncle attended to them and calmly offered one of them a drink in the manner I have already described above in order to see if these people, too, would waste the drink as the other two had done before. And, indeed, it happened just like before; they neither drank it nor concerned themselves with it. Having seen how little they minded his things, my uncle said, "If you disrespect me, I will also disrespect you."[15] He got up angrily and raised a cry as though he wanted to kill the Spaniards. However, the Spaniards were on the lookout and took possession of the four gates of the plaza where they were, which was enclosed on all its sides.

The Indians were thus penned up like sheep in this enclosed plaza, unable to move because there were so many of them. Also, they had no weapons as they had not brought any, being so little concerned about the Spaniards, except for the *lassos* and *tumës*,[16] as I have said above. The Spaniards stormed with great fury to the center of the plaza, where the Inca's seat was placed on an elevated platform, like a sort of fortress, which we call *usnu*.[17] They took possession of it and wouldn't let my uncle ascend but instead forced him out of his seat, turned it over and took away everything that he carried, as well as his tassel, which among us serves as a crown. After they had taken everything from him, they apprehended him, and because the Indians uttered loud cries, they started killing them with the horses, the swords or guns, like one kills sheep, without anyone being able to resist them. Of more than ten thousand not even two hundred escaped.[18] When all were dead, they took my uncle to a jail, where they kept him all night, stark naked and his neck in shackles. Next day, in the morning, they gave him his clothes and his tassel and asked, "Are you the king of this country?" He answered that he was, and they said, "There is none other beside you? For we know that there is another one called Manco Inca. Where is he?"[19] My uncle answered, "In Cuzco." They asked, "And where is that Cuzco?" My uncle replied, "Cuzco is two hundred leagues from here." The Spaniards in turn said, "We have learned that Cuzco is the capital of this country. Therefore he who resides in Cuzco must be the king." And my uncle said, "He is indeed, for my father willed that he would be, but because he is very young, I govern the country in his place." The Spaniards answered, "Even though he may be young, he should be notified of our arrival and that we have come on orders of Viracocha." My uncle said, "Whom do you want me to send after you have killed all my men and have left me in such a predicament?" He said this because he was not on good terms with my father and because he feared that once he [my father] was informed of the arrival of the Viracochas [Spaniards], the Spaniards might possibly get ahold of him, for they appeared to be powerful people, even Viracochas, as I have said above.

When the Spaniards saw that my uncle Atahuallpa procrastinated in informing my father of their arrival, they agreed among themselves to send their own messengers. Meanwhile, while the Spaniards were still deliberating whether or not to send the messenger, the Tallana people on the coast found out about the whole thing and, because they respected my father a great deal and acknowledged him as their king, decided to bring the news themselves to my father, without informing the Spaniards or my uncle. Thus they left for Cuzco and, upon their arrival, addressed my father with these words: "Sapai Inca" (which means "you, our sole lord"),[20] "we have come to tell you that a new sort of people [*género de gente*] has arrived in your land, a race that has never been heard of or seen before by our nations and that without doubt appears to be that of the Viracochas" (which means "gods"). "They have arrived at Cajamarca, where your brother is. He has told them in no uncertain terms that he is the lord and king of this country. This has caused us, as your vassals, great grief. As we are unable to stand such an affront any longer without informing you of it, we have come to warn you about what has been happening, for we would not want to give the impression that we are rebellious or negligent in our service to you."

When my father heard this, he was beside himself and said, "How dare those people intrude into my country without my authorization and permission? Who are those people and what are their ways?" The messengers answered, "Lord, these people cannot but be Viracochas, for they claim to have come by the wind.[21] They are bearded people, very beautiful and white. They eat out of silver plates. Even their sheep, who carry them, are large and wear silver shoes. They throw yllapas like the sky. From this you may yourself conclude that people like this, who live and behave in such a manner, must be Viracochas. Moreover, we have witnessed with our own eyes that they talk to white cloths by themselves and that they call some of us by our names without having been informed by anyone and only by looking into the sheets, which they hold in front of them. Finally, they are people whose only visible parts are their hands and their face. The clothes that they wear are even better than yours, for they contain gold and silver. Who could people of this manner and fortune be but Viracochas?"

My father, who was the type of man who wanted to know things for certain, turned to threatening the messengers, saying, "You better be sure that you haven't lied to me in any of the things you report, for you know very well how my ancestors and myself deal with liars."[22] The messengers, somewhat intimidated and terrified, spoke, "Sapai Inca, had we not seen it with our own eyes and hadn't we been concerned for you, we would never have dared to come to you with such stories. However, if you don't want to believe us, send someone to Cajamarca. Whoever you might send there will see the people we have described and who are waiting for an answer to our message."

When my father saw that they insisted so strongly on the veracity of what they had reported, he believed them and said, "If you are so eager to testify to the arrival of these people, why don't you go and bring one of them to me, so I can see them and thereby be persuaded." Thus, the messengers carried out what my father had ordered, returning to Cajamarca accompanied by a great number of Indians whom my father had sent so that they may verify what had been reported and in order to invite one of the Spaniards to come to visit my father, because he was very eager to see for himself such people as they had been described to him so earnestly by the Tallana people from the lowlands. At last all the messengers embarked from Cuzco for Cajamarca on command of my father in order to see what sort of people these Viracochas were. Upon their arrival, they were received very well by the Marquis Don Francisco Pizarro, who was most pleased about the news from my father and about some little trinkets—I am not sure exactly what—that he had sent. The messengers conveyed to the Spaniards my father's request that some of them might come see him. The Spaniards accepted the invitation and decided to send two of them in order to kiss his hands. One was named so-and-so Villegas and the other Antano. (The Indians did not know what to call them otherwise.)[23] Thus, they left Cajamarca upon command of the marquis and with the consent of the others and arrived in Cuzco without any delays or obstacles. My father, who had meanwhile been informed of their coming, sent them a great amount of supplies and even commanded the messengers who had come from Cuzco to meet them in order to carry them in hammocks, which they did. Once they had arrived in Cuzco, they were introduced to my father, who received them very respectfully and supplied them with shelter and everything they needed.

The next day, he invited them to his residence and hosted a great celebration with many people and much display of gold and silver dishes, among them innumerable pitchers, cups, bowls, and pots from the same material. When the Spaniards caught a glimpse of so much gold and silver, they told him to let them have some of it, so that they could show it to the marquis and his companions in order to demonstrate to them the greatness of his power. My father agreed and gave them many pitchers, golden cups, and other regalia and precious pieces for themselves and some for their companions. He sent them off with many people to accompany them and said that since they had come to see him on orders of Viracocha, they were welcome to enter his land and, if they so pleased, to visit him at his residence.

While these two Spaniards had been on their way to kiss my father's hands and to meet with him in Cuzco, my uncle Atahuallpa gave the Spaniards a huge amount of gold and silver, all of which belonged to my father.[24] He did this in part because he was afraid of the Viracochas and in part on his own design, because he was competing for their favor against Manco Inca, my father, and his brother, Huascar Inca. Because of his suspicion toward my uncle Huascar Inca, he sent out several messengers with the mission to instigate a conspiracy among Huascar's people in order to kill him, so that his back would be covered in that regard. With regard to the Spaniards, he was confident that he was safe because he had given them the treasure, which, as I have already said, belonged to my father. These messengers executed the plan very well, murdering Huascar during an altercation in the vicinity of a town called Huánuco Pampa.[25] When Atahuallpa found out about the death of Huascar Inca, he was exceedingly pleased, for he thought that he no longer had anyone to fear. On the one hand, he had destroyed and killed his main antagonist and, on the other, he had bribed the Spaniards. Thus, he thought he was safe. However, he was mistaken. When the two Spaniards arrived at the place where the Marquis Don Francisco Pizarro was staying with the messengers and the news that my father had sent, the marquis, whom we used to call *macho capitu*,[26] was assured that my father, Manco Inca Yupanqui, was the true king of the entire land—the one who was respected, feared, and recognized as such by all—while Atahuallpa, his older brother, ruled the land as a tyrant. The marquis was extremely delighted, either because he had the good news from my father of how high a person he was or because of the exquisitely beautiful and generous gift that my father had sent. But he was also upset by the news that my father's brother vexed and molested him so much without any reason and that he had usurped his kingdom in defiance of all laws. However, as it turned out later, Atahuallpa did not escape the punishment that he deserved.

When the Spanish messengers who had been at my father's court and the Indians whom my father had sent returned with the aforesaid treasure of gold and silver worth more than two million,[27] they presented it to the governor—first the Spaniards and then the Indians, just as my father had commanded. They said that Manco Inca Yupanqui was very glad about the arrival of so many good people in his land and requested that they come to his residence in Cuzco, if they pleased. He would receive them with all honors and promised to satisfy all their wishes, because they had come on order of Viracocha. He further wanted to inform them that at the place where they had landed there was one of his brothers by the name of Atahuallpa, who pretended to be lord of the entire land. They should not recognize him as such, because he [Manco Inca Yupanqui] alone was the legitimate ruler of the land, having been appointed as such by his father Huayna Capac in his last days. But despite his father's last will, Atahuallpa had risen up against him.

When the governor and all his people had heard all of this and more, he received the messengers of my father, as well as the presents, with great pleasure and ordered that they be shown the hospitality and honor appropriate for messengers of such a great lord. A few days later, the Indian messengers of my father embarked on their journey back with the response of the marquis, who remained in Cajamarca. Because of his suspicion, he continued to hold Atahuallpa prisoner, as he had done since he and his comrades had arrived in the land. For, it seemed to him that he [Atahuallpa] would rise up against him as soon as he released him. Also, he had always been suspicious of him, believing that he was not the legitimate king of the land but wished to gain certainty through the answer of my father. Thus, he kept him in captivity in order to await further instructions from my father.

When my uncle Atahuallpa saw that my father had sent messengers and so much gold and silver to the Spaniards, he was very upset. Not only was it not lost on him how quickly he [my father] had aligned himself with them and that they recognized him as the legitimate king and lord, but also he thought that this alliance would be his doom. As he was harboring this suspicion and fear of being thus cornered, he decided to summon all of his people and captains who were with him in order to apprise them of the sad condition in which he found himself. As soon as he had all of them gathered before him, he spoke to them the following words.

"*Apoes*" (which means "lords"),[28] "these people who have entered our lands hold notions contrary to our own and have aligned themselves with my brother Manco Inca and seem to live in great harmony with him. If you are in agreement, we will dash their heads in and kill them. For I believe that, although we have but few brave men, we can again rule this land the way we used to because my brother Huascar Inca is already dead. If we don't kill them, however, and they align themselves with my brother [Manco Inca], we will fare very badly because they are brave people—Viracochas apparently—and my brother is very angry at me. If he had a mind to summon troops from throughout the country, he would probably make these here [Spaniards] his captains, which means that he and they would invariably destroy us. So let us preempt them, if you agree."

The men and captains who had heard the reasoning of my uncle Atahuallpa agreed and cried in unison, "Hu Sapai Inca" (which means "you have spoken truly, lord").[29] "It is time to kill these people [the Spaniards], for what can they do against us? All of them together wouldn't even make a lunch for us." However, soon after they had determined the day and hour on which they wanted to carry out their plot, the marquis—I don't know how—found out about it. Thus, the marquis had them for lunch before they could have him, because he now knew about the conspiracy against the Spaniards. He positioned his spies everywhere and ordered highest alert. Without delay, he had my uncle Atahuallpa brought out of prison into the open and, without any resistance, garroted him on a pole in the middle of the square.[30] And as soon as this was done, he set out to depart in order to see my father. But no matter how quickly he acted, the Indians still came down upon him like a rainstorm, for an Indian by the name of Challcochima, Atahuallpa's general, and another by the name of Quisquis, his companion (both of whom were very brave and powerful), had gathered a great multitude of people to avenge the death of their lord. Thus, the marquis and his people were forced to proceed with great caution, because their pursuers were so numerous that they could advance only by suffering great troubles and damages. They constantly had to defend themselves against the overwhelming attacks.

When my father had news about the distress in which they found themselves, he decided to raise men who would rush to their aid. Thus, he departed from Cuzco with more than 100,000 people and came as far as Vilcacunga, where he met the marquis, who had already captured Challcochima. The marquis was very happy to see him [my father], who had traveled with his golden and crystal litters [andas] and his royal crown. He dismounted and embraced the marquis, who had already dismounted from his horse. My father and the marquis made an alliance with each other and ordered that nobody was to make a move unless it was to deal with Quisquis, who was roaming the vicinity with many people and who must not be allowed to succeed in freeing Challcochima.

After their meeting, my father and the marquis departed together from Vilcacunga and spent the night in Jaquijaguana, where the marquis turned over Challcochima to my father with the following words: "Look, lord Manco Inca, here I bring you your archenemy in chains. Decide for yourself what you want to do with him." When my father saw him, he ordered that he be burnt immediately before everyone's eyes,[31] so that this news would reach his ally Quisquis and, thus, be a punishment for the former and an example for the latter. After the punishment against so bad an Indian as he was had been executed, they [the marquis and Manco Inca] went together to Cuzco. Meanwhile, my father was still upset by the insolence of that Indian Quisquis. As soon as they arrived at Cuzco, my father commanded his people to show respect and esteem for the marquis and his people and to supply them with everything they needed until their return. He himself wanted to go and kill that villain Quisquis and his entire family, because he was so insolent toward him and the Spaniards. Then, my father respected the Spaniards a great deal, because he was very impressed by the Marquis Don Francisco Pizarro.

Manco Inca and the Captain Antonio de Soto[32] pursue Quisquis, traitor to His Royal Highness and to his King Manco Inca

The next day, after my father had supplied the marquis and his entire entourage with all things necessary, he decided, in consultation with the said marquis, to go after the traitor Quisquis, for he had been very angry with him since he had come to love and esteem the Spaniards. When the marquis saw how determined my father was to make this journey, he suggested taking part in this enterprise himself, pointing out that it wouldn't be right for him to stay back in the city while my father was going to war; for two together could effect more than one alone. My father acknowledged the marquis' offer but answered that for the time being he shouldn't move from the spot but rest and relax until his return, which would be very soon. If he wanted to send along a few men, he would be happy to take them with him. For the time being, however, he did not permit him to leave the city.

When the Marquis Don Francisco Pizarro saw that my father wouldn't let him leave the city and wouldn't take him along, he consulted with his captains. They thought that my father was right and chose Antonio de Soto to accompany my father. He took with him fifty Spanish soldiers. As soon as the said captain Antonio de Soto was chosen, the marquis went to the house of my father, who was already getting ready to leave, and apprised him of their decision. When my father learned of it, he was very glad and said that this decision was entirely right. Then he commanded the soldiers to get ready, for he wanted to depart.

On the same day, my father departed with all his people, accompanied by the captain Antonio de Soto and his followers, in order jointly to go after Quisquis. Only a few days' marches later, they caught up with the traitor Quisquis, whom they found in a village called Capi, fifteen leagues from Cuzco. They engaged in a merciless battle in the course of which they killed a great number of men and defeated him [Quisquis]. He himself abandoned his men in flight and was able to make his escape without anyone's notice. After my father and the captain Soto had thus defeated Quisquis and all his people, they returned to Cuzco but not without having assigned a great number of soldiers to pursue Quisquis and to bring him alive from wherever they found him.

Having returned to Cuzco after the defeat of Quisquis, my father and the captain Antonio de Soto were received very well by the Marquis Don Francisco Pizarro, his entourage, and the citizens of the city. The news of the victory over Quisquis and his army caused much joy and merriment. At the end of the welcome festivities my father retired into his chambers and the Spaniards into theirs. On the morning of the following day, my father summoned together all those who had returned with him from fighting Quisquis and those in the city who lived in my father's palace in order to feast with them. After the meal, he ordered that no one should dare to harass the newly arrived people, or [risk] losing his life; instead, they should respect and venerate them like a Viracocha, which means "God." He also commanded that they should provide them with servants, Indians, and people for their residence. My father himself selected a number of his own servants to serve them. When all of this was done, my father again equipped soldiers in order to pursue the traitor Quisquis, declaring that if necessary he would go to the ends of the earth in order to catch him and kill him because of his treason against him and the Viracochas.

My father supplied himself with everything necessary for the military campaign and left his brother Paullu, as well as Ticoc and other generals, in command in his place and of the government of the city. Then he took leave of the marquis with the vow that he would not return unless he had killed the traitor Quisquis. He left Cuzco the following day, accompanied by the captain Antonio de Soto and his men. After making steady progress in a march that lasted several days, they arrived at a town called Vinchu, fifty leagues from Cuzco, where they encountered the messengers who had been sent in pursuit of Quisquis after the battle of Capi. They reported that they had looked everywhere for the traitor but that they had been unable to find either traces or news of his whereabouts. His captains had perpetrated many raids, but there were no news about him.

My father was very upset by the report of the scouts and wanted to move on. Just then, however, he received letters from the marquis in which the latter described the loneliness under which he suffered in my father's absence and begged him to return. Because of his love for the marquis, my father began his return but not before having sent emissaries to all the parts where the traitor might be hiding in order to fight and kill him. The emissaries departed with orders not to rest until they had reached Quito, four hundred leagues away (where the wretch died, as will be reported below). Meanwhile, they [my father and his men] returned to Cuzco, where my father learned of the death of the traitor, who, after countless skirmishes in which he was involved and various defeats, had lost so many soldiers through death or captivity that his own army, reduced to virtually nothing, bitterly charged him of his treachery and treason against his king and beheaded him. My father, satisfied to learn of the death of that traitor Quisquis, rested a bit and then called upon all his people to pay a tribute for the Spaniards' sustenance. While the tribute was being collected, my father presented them with a great amount of treasure that had been given to him by his ancestors. The governor and his men received them most happily and gratefully.

How the Spaniards took Manco Inca Prisoner

When the Spaniards saw themselves so enriched, they wanted to return to their home country. But my father, who considered them to be newcomers to his country, did not want to let them go but told them that he still wanted the pleasure of their company and wanted to keep them in his country a while longer so that they could inform their own country adequately about his. They gladly accepted and chose an emissary with whom they sent a large portion of the treasure for the emperor Don Carlos. Thus, they spent many days in Cuzco in my father's company and enjoyed themselves thoroughly. But greed, so powerful in all men, overcame them so completely that they were seduced by the Devil [demonio], always a friend of all evil and enemy of virtue, to conspire and plot in secrecy how and by what means they would torment my father and extort a greater amount of silver and gold than what they had already extorted from him. When my unsuspecting father, a few days after this plot had been forged, was serenely staying in his house, more than a hundred Spaniards came with treacherous intentions under the pretext of paying him a visit. When my father saw them coming, he received them happily and gladly, for he was under the assumption that they had come to visit him, as they had many times before. But then, they executed their treason and arrested him saying, "We have found out, Manco Inca, that you are planning to rise up against us just like your brother Atahuallpa in order to destroy us. Be informed, however, that the governor has ordered us to arrest you and to put you in chains, so that you will be unable to harm us."

When my father saw them so determined, he was very upset and exclaimed, "What have I done to you that you should treat me in this manner and chain me like a dog? Is this how you reciprocate the favors I have done you by guiding you through my land and by making you many loving presents of things that I owned here? You are doing me very wrong. Are you not those who claimed to be Viracochas and emissaries of Tecsi Viracocha?[33] But it is not possible that you really are his sons, for you want to do evil onto those who have done you so much good. Have I not sent you a large amount of gold and silver to Cajamarca, and have you not taken from my brother Atahuallpa that which rightfully had been passed down to me by my ancestors? Have I not given you everything in this city that you desired, the sum of which equals a huge amount, more than six million? Have I not given servants to you and your subordinates and ordered the entire country to pay tribute to you? What more do you want me to do? Judge for yourself and you will see that I am right in my complaints."

The Spaniards, as though they were blinded by their evil greed, replied, "Whatever, *Sapai* Inca,[34] don't waste your breath by making excuses, for we have proof that you are intending to start an uprising in the entire land. Listen, men, bring some shackles." These were brought without delay and put on my father's feet, without any respect to his august person or to all the good things he had done for them. And when my father found himself thus bound he sadly said, "In truth, I tell you, you are devils [demonios], not Viracochas, for you treat me like this although I am innocent. What do you want?" The Spaniards answered, "Nothing for right now, except that you stay bound." Thus, they left him with a few guards and went back in order to report their actions to the governor, who was not entirely innocent in this affair. As my father found himself imprisoned in this manner, he was overcome by great sadness and he did not know what to do, for nobody except for his countrymen could console him. Finally, after some days—I don't know how many—Hernando Pizarro, Juan Pizarro, and Gonzalo Pizarro returned with many others and said to my father, "Senor Inca, are you still plotting an uprising throughout the land?" And my father said, "I am suspected of plotting an uprising throughout the land? What are you talking about? The land isn't even mine any longer, so how could I plot an uprising?" To this the Spaniards replied, "We've been informed that you've plotted to kill us and that's the reason why we've arrested you; however, if it is not true that you were plotting an uprising, it would be well if you redeemed yourself by giving us some gold and silver, for this is what we have come to seek. If you give it to us, we will set you free." Then Hernando Pizarro also said, "Although you may give us more gold and silver than would fill four bohíos,[35] I, for my part, will not let you go unless you first give me the lady coya,[36] who is your sister, by the name of Cura Oclo as my wife." This he demanded because he had seen her and fallen in love with her, as she was very beautiful. When my father saw them so determined in their bad intentions, he said, "So, that's what Viracocha commands you to do: to rob another man of his possessions and wives? With us, on the other hand, this is not customary behavior and I assert that you are not sons of Viracocha but of supai— which is to say the Devil in our language.[37] But so be it! I will try to find the things that you require." And they replied, "Don't think that it can be just anything. You will have to give us at least as much as you gave us upon our arrival; that was a treasure that wouldn't even have fit into the largest bohío that you Indians build, no matter how big it is." My father, as he saw them being so pushy and determined and as he didn't want to waste any more words, said, "Go on, I will do what I can and notify you." Still half dubious whether their design would work out, the Spaniards left. The next day, my father made an announcement throughout the land that the population was to gather and bring treasures in such amounts as the Spaniards demanded from him so insistently. When they had all gathered, he made the following speech.

Manco Inca Yupanqui's Speech to his people about the raising of the treasure which he handed over to the Spaniards during his first Imprisonment

"My brothers and sisters, a few days ago I had already had you gather in this way in order to introduce to you a new race [género] of people, which landed in our country. I am referring to those bearded ones who are now staying in this city. I did so because they claimed to be Viracochas[38] and because their clothes appeared to corroborate their claim. Then I commanded you to serve and venerate them as you would do for me personally and to pay tribute to them with whatever your region has to offer for I presumed that they were a grateful people and that they were emissaries of Him that, according to their words, appeared to be Teqsi Viracocha" (meaning "God").[39] "However, I now believe that I was mistaken in my assumptions. For you must know, my brothers, that they are the sons not of Viracocha but of the Devil [demonio], as they have proven to me time and again since they first arrived in this country. What they have done to me since their arrival, and are still doing to me, is evil, as you can see with your very own eyes. If you truly love me, you must feel great pain and sorrow when seeing your lord in chains and, without any wrongdoing on his part, so maltreated; only because I admitted such people to this county and, thus, put the noose around my own neck. If you want to do something for me, attempt, by your lives, to find a reasonable amount of gold and silver—for that is this what they covet—so that I can redeem myself from this pain and this captivity in which you see me now.

How the Indians responded to Manco Inca's call to gather a treasure while he was in captivity

Thus, a multitude gathered from the four parts of the land, which is more than 1,200 leagues long and almost 300 leagues wide and according to cosmography divided up into east, west, north, and south. We name these parts in circular order Antisuyu, Chinchaysuyu, Contisuyu, and Collasuyo, for Antisuyu refers to the east, Chinchaysuyu to the north, Cuntisuyu to the west, and Collasuyo to the south. This way of dividing up the land originated in Cuzco, the center and capital of the entire land. My ancestors, who lived there since the beginning, therefore called themselves the Lords of Tahuantinsuyu, which is to say "Lords of the four parts of the earth," for they were convinced that there was only this one world. For this reason, they always used to send messengers into the four parts, as my father also did for this aforementioned gathering, so that the entire population may come to the capital. Thus they communicated with the innumerable people, who came to the capital. Although many people had died at Cajamarca and during the chase for Quisquis, as well as during many other battles, which I will omit here for brevity's sake, more than ten thousand gathered, counting only the officials. When they were thus gathered before my father and saw him in such a miserable condition, they exclaimed with great sorrow, "Sapai Inca! Which heart in this world would not break and melt in lamentation at the site of our king suffering from such oppression and pain? To be sure, Sapai Inca, by admitting such people into the country, you have made a grave mistake. But since what happened has happened and cannot be changed now, we, your subjects, are prepared to do everything that you command us to do. Whatever it is that you might order us to bring, it is nothing next to all that we owe to you. If that of which you speak is not enough and it is necessary for us to sell ourselves, our wives, and our children in order to redeem you from your torment, we will readily do it to serve you. And know, our lord, whatever you may command us to bring will be done in due time and exactly as you have commanded, even if it means digging up the earth with bare hands."

When my father, Manco Inca, saw how eagerly his subjects wanted to serve him and to fulfill his wishes, he thanked them and said, "Truly, Apoes" (which means "lords"), "I am very obliged for your proven willingness to redeem me from the torment to which I am subjected by sacrificing yourselves and your possessions. I give you my royal promise that you will not regret it; [and] unless I die, I will make it up to you. All of this has been entirely my own fault, the result of letting such bad people into the country, and now I have to deal with it. You can do me a great favor by bringing the treasure quickly, because I am suffering very much from my captivity and maltreatment. In order to prevent those men from torturing me any longer, it is necessary that you fill that *bohío* there—by which he meant a great house—with gold and silver to the bursting. Perhaps, the sight of this will stop them from molesting me."

The generals and the other people replied in unison, "Señor Sapai Inca, that is nothing next to what we owe to you. It will be done as you command immediately." And thus, they all took leave in order to get what my father had demanded from them. After a short time, they returned with the desired things, which were piled up and arranged in accordance with my father's orders. The next day my father called for the Spaniards, who followed his call immediately.

How the Spaniards arrived at Manco's House while he was imprisoned and what happened after their Arrival

After the Spaniards had arrived at the place where my father was imprisoned and fettered, they greeted him as they had done on previous occasions and my father, too, paid them the customary respects when he saw that they had arrived and entered his house. He started the conversation by inquiring about the macho capito, who was not present at the time. Thus, he asked Hernando Pizarro, "Apo, where is the macho capito?" Hernando Pizarro replied that he had stayed at home, being ill; but my father, who wanted to see him, said, "Shouldn't we call him?" And Gonzalo Pizarro and the others replied, "As you wish, Manco Inca, call him here. It would be appropriate to call for him on your behalf." My father sent a few of his generals to call on him, but the governor replied that he was currently ill and that he would attend to my father's requests as soon as he felt better. When my father learned that he would not come, he addressed the Spaniards with the following words.

The Speech of the Imprisoned Inca to the Spaniards, as he handed over the first Treasure to them

"Gentlemen, for many days now you have been doing me great injustice by treating me the way you do, despite the fact that I did not give you any reason whatsoever, especially considering that I admitted you into my country, that I have received you with great honors and pomp in my city and my house, and that I have willingly let you have everything that I owned in my land and my house, which was, you may remember, not insignificant:

more than two million in gold and silver; more, as I know, than everything your king owns taken together. You know very well that it was in my hands whether or not to admit you into my country; for had I not wished it, you would not have been able to enter, even if there had been ten times as many of you as you are. You don't know how powerful the people of this country are and how many fortresses and troops there are. You would do well to remember my benevolence in inviting you, without you having to ask for it, and how I sent you everything I could as a token of friendship, because I had been informed that you were Viracochas, emissaries of Tecsi Viracocha. You would do well to remember that immediately after your arrival I provided you with servants and summoned the entire population of the land in order to call on them to pay tribute to you. And in gratitude for this, as well as for the devotion and benevolence I have shown you, you have imprisoned me and brought me into this situation, all on the pretext that I wanted to rise up against and kill you, although I never thought of anything like this. I know well that greed has blinded you and seduced you to commit such foolishness; that is the reason why you have mistreated me like this. I never would have thought that people who initially appeared in such positive light, and who even claimed to be sons of Viracocha, would become guilty of such acts. On your lives, release me and understand that I wish you no evil but only to please you. In order to satisfy your greed and the great hunger that you have for silver, you shall be given what you request. But beware that you receive it under the obligation not to torment and maltreat me and the entire population of this country. Don't think that I am handing these things over to you out of fear, for I am doing it voluntarily. Why should I be afraid? After all, the entire country is under my power and command. If it were my wish, my people could chase you out of the land in a very short time. And don't think that I am worried about the fetters with which you have kept me imprisoned. Had I wanted to, it would have been very easy for me to rid myself of them. But I didn't do it in order to make you understand that my conduct is inspired by love, not fear. That's why I have been dealing with you like this and will continue to deal with you as I have been. Let us keep the peace from now on and live in love and friendship. For you should know that it would greatly upset Viracocha" (which is to say "God") "and your king if it were to be any different. And I, too, wouldn't want it any differently."

When my father was finished with his speech, the Spaniards who had come with Hernando Pizarro, Gonzalo Pizarro, and Juan Pizarro thanked him for his words and even more for the gifts, namely the treasure and the other pieces of jewelry.

How the Spaniards thanked Manco Inca for the treasure and the Jewelry that he handed over to them at his Release

"Señor Manco Inca, all of us who are present here, as well as the lord governor Don Francisco Pizarro, know very well that we are indebted to Your Highness, who is the son of such a father as Huayna Capac, for our possession of the land that we now own and for the happiness and joy we feel about being here. If Your Highness were not what you are, which is a person of royal blood, we would not have the land that we now have and not the riches that we received by your generous hands. May it please our Lord the Almighty God (whom Your Highness calls Viracocha), our Father in his divine majesty, to requite the benevolence you have shown us and the good deeds you have done us by making you realize who His most Holy Majesty is. May your knowledge of Him make you love Him; may your love of Him perfect your knowledge of Him; and may your perfect knowledge of Him make you rejoice in Him and His Kingdom forever, as we, too, enjoy ourselves, having gotten to know the favors that Your Majesty has bestowed up us." Hernando Pizarro added on behalf of everyone, "All these noblemen and myself are most happy about the favors that Your Highness have shown us. We are now obliged for the rest of our lives to serve you and to assure you that we, these gentlemen and I, will not do you any harm, now or ever, provided we don't have a sufficient reason for it."[40]

After the Spaniards had thus addressed my father with this explanation and declaration of gratitude, he ordered the treasure to be turned over to them. They received it but left it untouched until they had reported to the governor everything that had happened. While some of them were waiting around, others immediately set out to get him, so that he could thank my father for the treasure and also so that he could be present at its reception and distribution. As it turned out later, it was only on account of the governor's request that the Spaniards had actually freed my father from his prison; had they not been ordered to do so, they wouldn't have done it. Thus, those who had gone to call him had done so in order to notify him that my father had already been released. As soon as he learned of what had happened and that my father had already been released, he came by. Upon his arrival, he greeted my father with the following words.

The Governor's Arrival at the House of Manco Inca

"May God preserve Your Highness, Señor Manco Inca. A minor illness has prevented me from coming earlier with these gentlemen to kiss your hands. It pained me greatly not being able to do what I so much desired, which is to meet with Your Highness. But this temporary absence, which, as I said, was due to my illness, will not happen again. I was very upset by the news of your arrest, especially in light of the possibility that it was entirely unjust, and my anguish will be even greater if it does turn out to be so. Indeed, as I am beholding these generosities of Your Highness, it now seems to me that this is precisely the case. As I always was and still am convinced of Your Highness's goodness, I have asked these gentlemen not to molest you so much. I am sure that a person who has brought us into his country with such goodwill and who has so plainly turned it over to us, with all of its treasures, could not be instigated so easily to do something that he shouldn't do. I entreat you, Your Highness, not to let the pain get the better of you, for these noblemen and I will do everything from now on not to cause you any more pain but, on the contrary, to pay you all the respect that is due to a person of the rank of Your Highness. It seems to me that Your Highness, now as then, are conducting yourself toward me and these gentlemen in the way we are used to, which is quite evident in the riches and treasure with which you have presented us, as well as in the share due to me in my function as governor, as well as the Royal Fifths, which is due to His Majesty. I kiss Your Highness's hand, for I know that His Majesty will be very pleased by what Your Highness has given here, which will add to what I already sent. For this favor, I am in your debt to a degree that I cannot express in words."

Manco's Answer to the Governor

"You are welcome, Apo" (which means "lord"). "I have longed to see you for many days, and I don't know why you wouldn't want to do me the favor. I desired to see you so much and called for you—I don't know how many times—in order to complain to you about your soldiers. But you have denied me this favor in order to please them, despite the fact that I desired and have done everything to please you. You have poorly requited my good intentions and my benevolence. Without any provocation on my part, these soldiers have tormented and hurt me by putting these iron fetters on me as though I was their llama" (which means "sheep" [*carnero*]). "It seems to me that this harassment is motivated more by greed than heroism. Obviously, I've been held prisoner more because of insatiable greed than because of any jurisdiction that they might rightfully claim over me. As you have seen for yourself and can testify, you [Spaniards] defeated me not by the force of arms but through pretty words. Had you not pretended to be sons and emissaries of Viracocha and had we not given any credit to the ingratiating devices that have brought to bear on me, I should like to know how you would have fared when entering our country. But because I conducted myself in the way I have done toward you, you treat me in this manner. Some noble recompense that you are giving me here for all the good things I have done for you! I don't even know how much gold and silver I paid your soldiers there in order to save myself from their harassment. But have it distributed as you see fit. And if you are a good Apo, you'll order them not to give me any more grief in the future, because I don't wish to give them any either; for let me assure you that they will regret it if they do." When the governor heard my father's answer, he was very pleased by it and commanded the Spaniards to receive the treasure, saying, "Let us receive what his Highness Señor Manco Inca Yupanqui has given us with such goodwill. Not only in this instance but for a long time now has he shown us great favors. And let's remember, gentlemen, that we have already received from him many things since we came into his country and that we have requited his generosity poorly. On your lives, from now on you shall pay him respect and high esteem, for he deserves it." Happy about the treasure that my father had given them, the soldiers responded to the governor with great joyfulness in the following manner.

The Answer of Hernando Pizarro, Gonzalo Pizarro, and Juan Pizarro, as well as the rest of the soldiers, to the governor

"Truly, Your Highness is entirely justified in reprimanding us and in decrying our conduct in this matter. Had there been a glimpse of consideration in us, we wouldn't have behaved in this manner but shown our gratitude to the person who had done us good. From now on, everything will be done the way that Your Highness commands." After all these declarations had been made by this, that, and the other Spaniard, they all went about dividing up the treasure amongst themselves, allotting to each what was due according to his rank. Hernando Pizarro was in charge of dividing up the treasure, for he was the one who had imprisoned my father. Because of the great quantity it would have taken too long to divide up the treasure by weight, so they divided it up in bags. When they had divided up the treasure amongst themselves, my father turned to the governor with the following words in order to express his gratitude.

"Apo, I believe that it was in part thanks to your influence that these soldiers have released me from an imprisonment that has turned out to be unjustified. I ask that you not rush off right away but that you dine with me as a sign of our pact of friendship. Let's have a collation together for I hope that what I have been promised will not be broken." In order to please my father and because this request was fair enough and not dangerous, the governor accepted. Thus, they all sat down in the hall where my father was and received the collation. When the pact had been sealed by this meal, everybody went home with the part of the divided treasure that had been allotted to him. It is believed that they accompanied the governor home and that each was very happy about his portion. However, as it turned out very soon, this happiness was not to last, for the Devil [demonio]—always evil and a friend of discord and disharmony—never rests.

The Rebellion of Gonzalo Pizarro against the Inca

According to what my father told me, less than three months later Gonzalo Pizarro was overcome by envy, which is the enemy of all goodness. On the one hand, it had occurred to him that the reason why his brother [Hernando] had received so much gold and silver was simply that he had taken my father prisoner to satisfy his greed while he was a corregidor [a royally appointed administrator]. On the other hand, he now found himself in possession of the power and command during the absence of the Marquis Don Francisco Pizarro, who had taken off for Lima with great protestations of his love and friendship for my father as well as on the best of terms with him. Gonzalo Pizarro, eager to demonstrate his power and authority at my father's expense, accused him of conspiring to rise up and kill them in their sleep at night. Under this pretext, he supplied himself with weapons and instigated Juan Pizarro and some others to take my father prisoner. Thus, they all went to the building where my father and his people were enjoying themselves during a celebration that was going on at the time. Upon their arrival, they were welcomed very benevolently and sincerely by my father, who was entirely ignorant of the impending conspiracy. But they, who were entirely possessed by their insidious intentions, waited until he had to go home for some reason and then followed him. Just as he was about to leave his house again, they seized him, whereupon Gonzalo Pizarro spoke the following words.

Manco's Inca's Second Imprisonment by Gonzalo Pizarro

"Señor Manco Inca, A few days ago, you and my brother Hernando Pizarro made an agreement that you would neither plot nor have any dealings in any more conspiracies. But it seems to me that you have not kept your promise, for we have received intelligence that you have gathered many people with the intention of attacking us by night. In the king's name, give yourself up as a prisoner; and don't think that this time you'll get off as easy as last time, when you proclaimed that you didn't mind the chains.

Now you can see for yourself whether they can be broken or not." Gonzalo Pizarro swiftly ordered that some fetters and a chain be brought and put upon my father. When my father saw that they wanted to put him in fetters and chains and realized the fate to which he was condemned, he tried to defend himself with the following words.

Manco Inca's Answer

"What sort of game are you playing with me? Are you mocking me at every turn? Do you not know that I am a son of the sun and a son of Viracocha, as you claimed to be? Do you think that I am just any person or some Indian of the common sort? Do you want to scandalize the entire country and be hacked to pieces? Do not mistreat me, for I have not given you any reason. Do you think I care about your fetters? I couldn't care less about them than I do about the ground I step on with my feet."

When Gonzalo Pizarro and his lieutenants saw my father so furious, they all threw themselves upon him in order to put the chain around his neck. They said, "Don't try to resist us, Manco Inca. Rest assured that we will tie your hands and feet so well that all the people of the world will not be able to free you. We are arresting you in the name and on behalf of the emperor, not on our own behalf. But were it on our own behalf, now you will hand us over much more gold and silver than last time; also, you will give me the señora coya Cura Oclo, who is your sister, as my wife." Thus, all who were present immediately put the chain around my father's neck and feet.

Manco Inca's Speech during his second Captivity

When my father found himself arrested and chained in such a shameful and degrading manner, he spoke following words. "Am I a dog, sheep, or some sort of *oyua* [beasts of burden], so that you

-87-

have to put chains on me in order to prevent me from escaping? Am I a thief or have I committed treason against Viracocha or your king? Far from it! Why then, if I am neither a dog nor some other such creature, do you treat me like this? Truly, I say to you and insist upon it: you are more like the sons of supai than servants, let alone sons of Viracocha. For if you were not even the sons but at least the servants of Viracocha, you would not treat me the way you do but be mindful of who I am and whose son I am, as well as of how great my power has been and still is, even though I have given it up out of consideration for you. Moreover, you would do well to remember that since your arrival nothing in this country — great or small, high or low — has been refused you. On the contrary, whereas I used to have riches, now you own them; whereas I used to command the people, now you are served by them, men and women, old and young, even children; whereas I used to have land, now the best that there is in this country is in your possession. Is there anything in this world that I didn't provide for you when you needed it? You certainly are ungrateful and deserving of being humiliated."[41]

Gonzalo Pizarro and Juan Pizarro, as well as the others who had accompanied them, did not pay any attention to the words my father had spoken to them and only remarked somewhat contemptuously, "Just calm down, calm down, Señor Sapai Inca, and relax a bit, for you are very agitated. Tomorrow we'll have plenty of time to talk about it. Just make sure that you give all the necessary orders so that much gold and silver will be accumulated." "And don't forget to hand over the coya," Gonzalo Pizarro said, "for I desire very much to have her." After the Spaniards had given my father such good consolations, they went to their houses to eat, for this capture had happened in the morning. However, before they disappeared in their houses they left a good guard to watch my father. Meanwhile, all the people who had been gathered in the plaza, called Puma Qurco, from where my father had left that morning during the communal meal in order to take care of something at home before being seized by the Spaniards, rushed by in great dismay to the building where my father was in order to see why he had not returned to the plaza in all the time that had passed. When they arrived at the door, they met one of my father's servants, all of whom were very upset by the arrest of their master and almost in tears. The leaders and other persons who had rushed by in order to learn what was happening were dumbfounded, making great lamentations and asking one another in bewilderment, "What is this? What is this?" In great alarm, the principal leaders of the entire country made their way to the interior of the house in order to ascertain what was happening and to see about my father. Having advanced to the inside of the house, for which they were given permission (otherwise nobody was allowed to enter), they reached the place where my father was imprisoned in the manner described above. When they saw him like this, they all broke into loud lamentations, which must have been quite a scene. One of them by the name of Vila Oma, who governed the entire land as the supreme commander on behalf of my father,[42] spoke in a loud voice to all who were present and then, trying to control himself,[43] turned to my father.

"Sapai Inca, what are these Viracochas designing to do? Today they take you prisoner, tomorrow they release you. They seem to be playing a silly game with you. However, I am not surprised that they treat you in this manner. You have brought it upon yourself by allowing such insidious people into the country without first asking our opinion. I tell you, if you had left me to deal with them when they first arrived at Cajamarca, they would have never made it to where you are now, for I and Challcochima, with the help of our faithful troops, would have prevented them from entering the country, regardless of what they wanted to do. I don't think that we would have fared as poorly as we did as a result of you being good. If you only hadn't told us that they were Viracochas and emissaries of Atun[44] Viracochan" (which means "the great God" [*gran dios*]), "and if you hadn't ordered us to obey and respect them as such, as you did yourself, we wouldn't have to endure the torments and molestations that are now happening to us. We are losing our possessions, our women, our sons and daughters, our fields; we are becoming the subjects of people we don't even know. We are being so oppressed and tormented that we are even forced to clean the dirt of their horses with our capes. Look, my lord, how deeply we have sunken into humiliation because this is the way you wanted it. So don't marvel at being treated this way, for this is what you wanted. You know very well how I tried to hold you back when you wanted to meet them at Vilcacunga and how often I warned you not to allow them to enter into your country. Moreover, if you would remember, as soon as we had news that they had arrived in our lands, I offered to catch up with them in a quick march with ten or twelve thousand Indians and to hack them to pieces. But you never permitted me to act: 'Quiet! Quiet! They are Viracochas, or sons of Viracocha.' As though we hadn't guessed that people of their kind, who came from distant lands, had more likely come to rule than to obey. We all, I and your people, are very upset about what has happened and feel great sympathy for you when seeing you like this. Give me your permission, so you can see that I haven't changed, and I will free you and destroy these beard-faces in no time at all. You still command enough people who will help me with this. As you know very well, in the entire land—upper, lower, and across—nobody save yourself commands greater respect than I, who am the supreme commander over all." After the captain Vila Oma had related the above to my father, he, along with another chief by the name of Ticoc, his companion, turned to the Spaniards who were present at the time, saying the following words to them with changed and severe expressions on their faces.

How the Inca's chiefs reprimanded the Spaniards for their poor treatment of their king and lord

"What sort of game are you playing here every day with our Inca? Today you arrest him; tomorrow you torment him; and the day after that you shower him with contempt. What has this man done to you? Is this how you requite the benevolence he has shown you by allowing you into the country against our will? What do you want from him? What else can he still do for you after everything he has already done? Did he not permit you to enter into this country in peace [with] great calm? Did he not greatly honor you by sending emissaries to call on you at Cajamarca? Did he not send off your emissaries with great honors, giving them great amounts of gold and silver and a large entourage? Did the Spaniards not travel in hammocks carried by his men? Did you not appropriate two of his houses full of silver and gold in Cajamarca, not even to mention Atahuallpa's presents—which also originally belonged to my Inca—and the great amount of silver and gold that he sent to Cajamarca from here? Were you not treated well in all during the 130-league journey from Cajamarca to this city and supplied with plenty of porters? Did he not himself come six leagues to meet you at Jaquijaguana? Did he not shortly after your arrival burn the most elevated personage in the entire country, Challcochima, out of consideration for you? Did he not give you houses and resting places, servants and women, as well as sown land? Did he not call upon the entire population to pay you tribute? Did they not deliver the tribute? Yes, yes, and yes! And the other day when you seized him, did he not finally give you a house full of gold and silver in order to redeem himself from his pains? Did you not take the wives, sons, and daughters from our dignitaries and common people? And we kept quiet about it all, because he thought it was the right thing to do and because we didn't want to hurt him. Do our people not continue to serve you by cleaning the dirt of your horses and houses with their own capes? What more do you want? Did he not acquiesce every time you said, 'Give us more gold, give us more silver? Gather this, gather that?' And did he not even give you his own servants in order to wait on you? What more do you desire from this man? Did you not betray him when you claimed that you had come with the wind on behalf of Viracocha and that you were his sons, that you wanted to serve and love the Inca and to treat him and all of his people just like you would your own? You know all too well—and if you care enough to look, you will see for yourself—that you have failed to live up to your word in all respects and that, instead of treating him the way you promised that you would, you harass him without any reason and continue to violate every credo, without having been given the slightest reason in the world.

"From where, do you think, is he supposed to get the gold and silver that you now demand, after he already handed over to you everything that was to be had in this country, including our jewelry? What is he supposed to give now in order to redeem himself from this current captivity? Where and how is he supposed to get what you demand? He has nothing left, nothing left to give. Your conduct has left all inhabitants of this country so outraged and disturbed that they don't know what to say and where to flee; for they find themselves deprived not only of their king but also of their wives, children, houses, things, lands—in short, all their possessions. Indeed, their misery is so great that they are often driven to hang themselves or to bash everything to pieces, as has often been reported to me. Therefore, gentlemen, it seems right to me that you should finally leave my Sapai Inca alone, for you are the cause of his distress and torment, and that you should free him from his present imprisonment, so that these Indians may be redeemed from their great distress."

The Spaniards' Reply to Vila Oma

"Who has commanded you to speak with such authority to the corregidor of the king? Do you have any idea what sort of people we Spaniards are? You had better be quiet! Otherwise, I'll swear by the life of His Majesty that if I get ahold of you, I will teach you and your companions a lesson that you'll remember for the rest of your life. If you won't shut up, I swear that I'll burn you alive and hack you to pieces. Who has ordered him, I ask, to speak with such air before me?" Gonzalo Pizarro said this in order to intimidate Vila Oma and the others who were present. Then he turned to retort what had been said, beginning: "You had better stop this and hurry up to gather the silver and gold, as I have ordered you. Otherwise, I swear to you that your king will not leave this prison until everything has been gathered, even if it takes a year. So stop arguing with me and don't tell me any stories about heroic deeds: from here he went, and from over there he came." After these things had passed between the Spaniards and the chief Vila Oma, the Spaniards left him and went to their houses, while he approached my father in order to report to him in detail what he had told them and what they had answered. When my father learned of the condition of his people and how much they shared in his torment, he said the following: "My sons and brothers, I know that I am paying the price for having permitted these people to come into this land; and I can understand why you have complaints about me. But since there is now no other remedy, on your life, gather something very quickly that will redeem me from these heavy torments. Of course, it is painful for you to see your king a prisoner, like a dog with a chain around his neck and like a slave or fugitive with fetters on his feet." The chiefs and the others, overcome by great compassion in the face of the maltreatments to which my father was subjected, did not know what to say but one after another went out the door, silently and with downcast eyes, in order to gather to the best of their ability what my father had commanded, so that he might soon be liberated. But despite their efforts, it took more than two months until they had gathered everything they could find. They even took one another's jewelry and the clothes that they wore. The number of people who gave things turned out to be so great that a large house was filled to the top with things. It included also some dishes that had been left in my father's house for his use. Finally, everything had been gathered under the great harassment perpetrated by those men, who continuously annoyed my father with words such as: "Is that all? That's not enough silver! How much longer will you make us wait? It is about time you finish!" Eventually, he called his people and told them to go and get the Spaniards, for he wanted to turn over to them what had been gathered, so that they would stop tormenting him. Thus they came, and as soon as they arrived where my father was, they greeted him and said, "May God preserve you, Señor Sapai Inca, what do you want? Why have you called for us?" Thereupon my father, who knew that he would soon be released, spoke to the Spaniards.

Manco Inca's Speech to the Spaniards

"Apocona"[45] (which means "sirs"), "when you recently imprisoned me for the second time, I said that you were not Viracochas; for if you were, you would not treat me so poorly after I only meant, and continue to mean, to do good things for you (and I gave you the reasons for this). Now, after you have aggravated my torment in such a grave and impious manner—for more than two months now, I have been chained here like a dog—I can't help but say this: not only have you not acted like Christians and sons of Viracocha, from whom you claim descent; rather, you have acted like servants of supai. You walk in his footsteps by doing evil to those who have done you well. You are even worse than he, for he covets neither silver nor gold because he needs them not. But you seek it; and where it is not to be had, you try to get it by force. You are worse than the Yuncas, who for a little precious metal would murder father and mother and deny the entire world. Likewise, you, too, failed to remember all the good things you have received from me. While I have loved you with so much fondness and have desired your friendship, you have let me down for a little silver and treated me worse than a dog for its sake, which leads me to believe that you care more about silver than the friendship of all the people in the world. In any case, because of your love of silver you have failed me and all of the people of my country; and because of your impunity and boundless greed, we—they as well as I—have been deprived of our jewelry and wealth, which you have taken from us by way of violence, torments, and harassments. But I tell you that it is my sense that you will not reap glory from the fact that you took, without right and reason, what those poor Indians have gathered with great toil. But be that as it may, take these things and finally set me free to leave this prison." My father said all of this with great anguish and even with tears in his eyes, considering the poor treatment to which he had been subjected.

How the Spaniards wanted to release Manco Inca from his second Imprisonment

Having heard what my father had said, the Spaniards, being very joyful and delighted about the accumulated silver, told him that they were very pleased with him. But when they seemed to be about to release him, which was only a trick, Gonzalo Pizarro suddenly appeared and said, "Not so fast! Don't set him free! First he has to give us the lady coya, his sister, whom we saw the other day. Why do you rush to set him free without ordering him to do so? Let's go, Señor Inca, let's have the lady coya! As far as the silver is concerned, you're fine, because that's what we primarily wanted."

How the Coya was turned over

When my father saw the importunity with which they demanded the coya and realized that he would not be able to get around this matter, he had a very beautifully dressed and adorned Indian woman presented to be turned over in place of the coya whom they were demanding. When the Spaniards saw her but did not recognize her as the coya, they said that this woman did not seem to them to be the coya but some other Indian woman, that he had better turn over the coya and stop this sort of trickery. My father, in order to lure them, had more than twenty others brought in a similar fashion, each one more beautiful than the next, but none satisfied them. Then, when the time seemed right to my father, he had a woman brought, the highest-ranking one in his house, the companion of his sister the coya, who looked very much like her, especially when she dressed like her, and who was called Ynguill—which means "flower"—and he gave her to them.[46] She appeared in the presence of all, robed and made up just like a coya—which means "queen."[47] And when the Spaniards saw her appear this way in all her pomp and beauty, they said with much enthusiasm and satisfaction, "That's her! That's her! That's the coya and none of the others." Gonzalo Pizarro, who desired her more than the others and had pursued her with particular persistence, said the following words to my father: "Sir Inca, if she is for me, let me have her now because I cannot wait any longer." And my father, who had initiated her well, said, "Very well then, do what you desire." And so, before everyone's eyes and without seeing anything else, he went up to her in order to kiss and embrace her as though she were his legitimate wife. This made my father laugh and the others wonder, while it greatly terrified and appalled Ynguill. As she saw herself being grabbed by a man whom she did not even know, she began screaming like a mad person, saying that she did not want to give herself to such people, that she would rather run away, and that on no account would she have them. Although

my father saw how recalcitrant she was and how much she resisted going with the Spaniards, he knew that his redemption
depended on her; so he furiously ordered her that she should go
with them. And when she saw my father so upset, she did what
she was ordered to do and went with them, more out of fear
than anything else.

How Gonzalo Pizarro received the treasure and the coya from the hands of Manco Inca and how he went to eat with him as a sign of friendship

After Gonzalo Pizarro received her, he ordered the fetters to be
taken off my father. When he [my father] was freed, they took
the treasure and distributed it among themselves. Once that was
done, Gonzalo Pizarro said to my father that, since he had given
so many things—in gold as well as silver, and above all the lady
coya, whom he had so desired—he would be honored to host
him and his noblemen at his house. There, he said, he would
now always be welcome, as a sign of the friendship that would
last for a long time between the two as a result of their now
being brothers-in-law. My father, because he wanted to go outside and see the land, as well as to make him happy, did what
Gonzalo Pizarro asked of him and went with him and his companions in order to eat at his house, where they had a great
celebration and merriment. He thought that this way the friendship with the Spaniards would be durable. After they had dined
together, my father said that he wanted to return to his house
because it was already late, and the Spaniards accompanied him
there and left him there very happy before they returned to their
own houses. (It should be pointed out to the reader that while
these things regarding the coya and the imprisonment with chains
and fetters were happening, the Marquis Don Francisco Pizarro
was in Lima and thus away from Cuzco at the time. Therefore,
nobody should think that he had any part in this.)

A few days after all these things had passed regarding the second imprisonment and the giving up of Ynguill instead of the coya to Gonzalo Pizarro, the latter—or I should rather say my father—held a very major festival. This festival, during which the ears are pierced, is the most important one that we Incas observe during the entire year, because it is the occasion of the Great Naming, when we receive a new name in place of the old one. It is a ceremony not unlike that of the Christians' confirmation.[48] In accordance with our customs, my father appeared at this celebration with all the regalia of royal authority and went in the lead of the procession carrying the royal scepters, one of which—the main one—was made of solid gold and ornamented with tassels made of the same material. Each of the others who accompanied him carried his own scepter, each of which was half silver and half copper. There were more than a thousand in total,[49] between these and those who came to be rebaptized, who are called *vacazoc*,[50] according to our tradition. Thus, all our Indians and the Spaniards were gathered on the plain before the hill called Anauarque, where this ceremony used to be celebrated. At the end of the ceremony—its course will be described in more detail later—when those who had been rebaptized went to wash[51] after they had been shaved and their ears pierced, the Spaniards, either because of their greed for the silver that was laid into the scepters or because of some suspicion caused by the appearance of so many people, drew their weapons and began to agitate all the people. They drew their swords with the following cry: "Oh, you villains! You want to make an uprising? But it won't come to that! Just wait, just wait!" And thus, they rushed for the scepters in order to take them away from those who were carrying them. They also desired to get to the one carried by my father, but because he had surrounded himself with a strong guard whose armor prevented them from getting to him, they just took what they could from the others, which was a lot. When my father heard all that noise and commotion among the people he tried to see what was happening. When he found out how impudently the Spaniards had conducted themselves, he raised his voice and said, "What is this?" And the Indians, almost weeping, complained with these words: "Sapai Inca, what sort of people are these whom you are hosting in your land? All the gold and silver that you have given them was not enough for them, so now they have violently taken away our silver *yauris*" (which means "scepters").[52] "They took them from us with threats, and we are very upset by this. Tell them to return them to us and to content themselves with the silver and gold that we have given them." And my father, who saw all the anguish with which those Indians complained, felt their pain and addressed the Spaniards in the following manner:

The Inca's Attempt to Reason with the Spaniards when they were about to take him Prisoner for the third time

"Gentlemen, it seems that you are still set on giving me and my people grief, although I have not wished to give you any and still do not wish you any. Did you not the other day promise me and my people that you would not give me any more pain? You have no right, for I have done nothing to you that would give you any reason. Don't you have enough silver yet, so that now you must take from me the little I have left for use in my ceremonies? Just tell me now if you are doing this in order to provoke me or the people to rise up against you. If so, I will be prepared, and so will my people; only this time, I will not be as carefree and unsuspecting as I have been before. If not, let's keep our promise—for we did give each other our word in the house of Apo the other day that we would live in peace and love with one another, so that you will not have any suspicions, nor we fear." When the Spaniards had heard what my father had said, they replied, "Señor Manco Inca, we do not want to give Your Majesty any pain. Some soldiers created a bit of a fuss in order to pass time. That's all. You are not suffering any pain." When my father saw that the people had calmed down and relaxed, he was quiet and finished his ceremony while the Spaniards went home, for it was already late and time to go to sleep.

The Death of Pascac, the Inca's brother

After all these festivities and other things related above had passed, my father, while he was peacefully resting in his house, learned of the progress of a bold conspiracy. One of his brothers, the somewhat arrogant Pascac, had the idea—I don't know who may have instigated him to it—to murder my father so that he could himself be king. Somebody—I am not sure whether it was the same person or persons who impressed him with this idea or somebody else—gave him a dagger with which he armed himself and went to see my father under the pretense that he had come to kiss him as a sign of his reverence to his lord. His real intention, however, was to stab him with this dagger and then, after my father's death, to become king and give much silver to the Spaniards; for it was them who had given him the dagger to this end. But, as there are no secrets that won't be revealed sooner or later, a certain Spaniard, whose name is not known but who was in my father's service and always stayed at his house, warned my father, "Beware, Señor Manco Inca, for your brother Pascac is coming to murder you. For this purpose he has hidden beneath his cape a dagger with which he is supposed to stab you while paying his respects to you with a kiss. Therefore, when you see him coming take heed and command me to kill him, and I will do so." Thus warned by his Spanish servant, my father thanked him very much and braced himself for seeing his brother come to visit and pay his kiss of reverence, as on previous occasions. When he saw him, he let him approach to pay his kiss and then stabbed him several times with a dagger that he had himself obtained for that purpose. The Spaniard who had warned my father gave him the coup de grace. All those who were present, upon seeing all of these events, were very much astonished to witness such strange and unexpected things, but nobody dared to say a word.

All these things happened and many more, but since an extended account of all of them would lead us too far astray and in order to avoid prolixity, I will stay on track by moving on to relate the things that happened to my father and the things that the Spaniards went about after all of this. When Gonzalo Pizarro (who was acting as the corregidor of Cuzco in the absence of the governor Francisco Pizarro), as well as Hernando Pizarro, Juan Pizarro, and many others were staying in the city, it happened that Juan Pizarro, the brother of Hernando Pizarro, found out about how much silver my father had given to his brothers and called out in a fit of envy, "So, only my brothers get silver, but not I? By the devil, that is about to change! They'll have to give me gold and silver as well, the same as they gave to my brothers. If they don't, I'll teach them a lesson that they won't forget." With these threats, he gathered all the people and said, "Let's arrest him, let's arrest Manco Inca." When my father learned that in the city there was a conspiracy being planned against him, he ordered that all the chiefs of the land come together. Actually, many of them were already in Cuzco for the protection of his person. When he had them all gathered before him, he, after having consulted with the above-mentioned chief Vila Oma, gave them the following speech.

The Inca's Speech to his Chiefs about the Siege of Cuzco

"My much beloved sons and brothers, I never thought that I would find myself compelled to require of you what I am about to; for I thought and always took for granted that these bearded people whom you call Viracochas would never deceive or harm me, for I used to think and say that they had indeed come on orders of Viracocha. Now, however, I look back on my experiences with them and discover—as you have seen—how badly they have treated me and how poorly they have thanked me for all that I have done for them. They have disrespected me a thousand times; they have taken me prisoner and chained my hands and feet like you would a dog; and, not enough, after they have promised me that they would from now on respect our compact of mutual love and friendship, they are now engaged in a plot to capture and kill me. So now I will ask you, like one asks one's sons, to remember what you have so often urged me to do, which is precisely what I want to do now: you said that I should rise up against them and you asked why I tolerated them in my country. So far, I have been reluctant to do so because I deemed it impossible that the things would happen that I now see happening. But because this is the way it is and because they insist on vexing me, I find myself compelled to do them likewise. I will not tolerate any more of their chicaneries. On your lives, you have always shown me much love; and you did your best in fulfilling my wishes. Now, fulfill only this one and gather all that are here. Get ready to send your messengers all over the land, so that in twenty days' time all are united here in this city but without the knowledge of those bearded ones. Meanwhile, I will send messengers to Lima, to Quiso Yupanqui, my captain who governs that region, in order to inform him that on the day that we attack these Spaniards who are here, he is also to attack those Spaniards who are there. Thus, if he acts there at the same time as we act here, we will finish them off without any of them staying alive; and we will rid ourselves of this nightmare and will be happy thereafter." After he had finished explaining his plan to his captains about how to get their men ready for the impending battle with the Spaniards, they all replied in unison and with one voice that they were very glad, willing, and ready to carry out what my father had ordered them to do. Thus, without further delay, they went to work as each sent envoys to the region that he controlled. From the Chinchaysuyo, Vila Oma sent Coyllas, Osca, Coriatao, and Taipi, so that they would mobilize the men from that region. From the Collasuyo, Llicllic went with many others in order to mobilize the men from that region. Surandaman, Quicana, Suri Uallpa, and many other captains went to the Cuntisuyu and Ronpa Yupanqui and many other captains into the Antisuyu. They all went to their respective regions in order to recruit the men necessary for the task at hand. (Remember that these four suyos that I have mentioned are, as I have explained in more detail above, the four parts into which this whole land is ordered and divided.) After these men had been sent out to the aforementioned regions and while the said Juan Pizarro roamed the land in a dangerous manner and with bad intentions, an Indian by the name of Antonico, who spoke the Spaniards' language, came to see my father and informed him that Juan Pizarro and the others wanted to arrest him the next day and even to kill him, unless he gave them much gold and silver. When my father heard what the said Indian [Antonico] told him, he believed him and made a pretext of going out to Callca to hunt. The Spaniards, who were clueless as to what my father was planning to do, had no objections and thought that they could carry out their evil design after his return, which they thought would be soon.

After my father had stayed in Callca for a few days and while the men whom he had sent for were gathering, he sent a dispatch from there via a courier[53] to Quiso Yupanqui in Lima in order to inform him of the day and hour in which he was planning to attack the Spaniards, so that he, too, would attack them and that, thus, both attacks—Quiso Yupanqui's in Lima and my father's in Cuzco—would be carried out at the same time. As my father was busy with these things, the Spaniards sent him many letters in which they asked him to return home soon for, they said, they missed him very much. My father replied by saying that he was not finished hunting but that he would return as soon as he could. As the Spaniards realized that whenever they sent for him he did not want to return and that day after day he procrastinated more and sent ever less credible replies, they decided to go after him in order to bring him back by force or to kill him. They appointed some captains in Cuzco and while some of them went out to effect the said objective, the others stayed back in Cuzco ready to reinforce the first group if necessary. They arrived at the bridge over the Callca River, where they were engaged by some guards who were blocking their passage. The Spaniards began to fight my father's men but then returned to Cuzco, followed by many of my father's men, who were uttering many shrieks and loud shouts. On their retreat to Cuzco, the Spaniards were a bit shaken by the battle that had passed and the people who were pursuing them. When the Spaniards reached Carmenga, which oversees all of Cuzco, they called upon the help of their comrades, whose vigilance had not relented and who rushed to the support of those in distress. At the said town of Carmenga, they engaged in battle with the pursuers and many others who had come there in answer to my father's call. The outcome of the battle was that the Indians cornered the Spaniards in Cuzco without killing many of them. During the night, they kept them locked in and on edge with loud cries. However, they did not attack them because they were awaiting the many men who were supposed to arrive the next day and also because my father had ordered them not to attack. He had given that order not only because he wanted to take them more easily once the reinforcements had arrived but also because he wanted to negotiate with them.

The Siege of Cuzco

The following day, after they had withdrawn to Cuzco in this manner, they put up many well-equipped guards overnight at all the entrances. In the evening, a tumultuous crowd arrived near Cuzco. However, they did not attack the city because they thought that the night had advanced too far and that the great darkness would not permit them to overwhelm their enemies. Thus, they erected camps on all the elevated points and mountains that allowed them to overlook the city and placed a great number of guards and sentries all around the camps. In the morning of the following day,[54] at nine o'clock, all the Spaniards were gathered in formation on Cuzco's central plaza (their precise number is unknown but it is said that they were numerous and that they had many blacks with them). Suddenly, a huge number of men appeared everywhere around Cuzco and closed in on the city with much noise and music from their whistles, horns, and trumpets, as well as loud war cries. Their number was so great that the whole world appeared to darken; there must have been more than four hundred thousand advancing in the following order.

The Indians' Advance in the Siege

From Carmenga, which lies in the direction of the Chinchaysuyu, came Coriatao, Cuillas, and Taipi, with many others in order to close the city's exit in that direction with their hordes. From the Cuntisuyu, which is the direction of Cachicachi, came Huaman Quilcana, Curi Huallpa, both superbly equipped and in battle formation, closing a huge gap of more than half a league wide. From the Collasuyu came Llicllic and many other generals with a huge number of men, which was in fact the largest contingent that formed the besieging army. From the Antisuyu came Antallca and Ronpa Yupanqui and many others in order to close the ring around the Spaniards. The impermeability of the completed ring was remarkable. They wanted to attack the Spaniards on that very day but did not dare to proceed as long as my father had not given the orders. For, as I have already explained, he had forbidden anyone, under penalty of death, to make a move. When

Vila Oma, the commanding general of the forces, saw all of them completely ready, he sent word to my father, who was staying at Callca at that time, to let him know that the Spaniards were surrounded and in great distress and to inquire whether they should kill them or do something else with them. My father replied that they should be left in their predicament; after all they, too, had caused him much grief, so they should suffer like he suffered. He would get there the next day and finish them off. When Vila Oma heard the message that my father sent him, he was very unhappy about it, for he would have preferred to destroy the Spaniards right away, as he could very easily have done. But he did not dare to disobey the will of my father and announced all around the place that, under penalty of death, nobody was to make a move until he had given the appropriate orders. Moreover, he had all the canals of the city opened in order to flood the fields and roads inside and outside the populated area in case that the Spaniards were to attempt a getaway. This way, they would find the entire land flooded and, once their horses got stuck in the mud, they would easily be overcome by their enemies on foot, for people dressed like the Spaniards have a difficult time in dealing with swamps. All of Vila Oma's orders were carried out exactly as he had commanded. When the Spaniards saw themselves thus surrounded and in such distress, they became convinced that their doom was imminent and, as they could not find a way out, they did not know what to do. While they found themselves so dangerously surrounded, they had to endure the Indians showering them with scorn and mockery, throwing stones on the roofs of their tents and mocking them by lifting a leg at them.[55] Moreover, the Indians began setting the Spaniards' shelters on fire and almost succeeded in setting ablaze the church during one of the raids, if it hadn't been for some blacks who were hiding on the roof. Although they had to endure a hail of arrows shot by the Sati and Anti Indians, they remained unharmed, being protected by God and their shields. As the Spaniards thought themselves lost in such a miserable situation, they entrusted their fate to God. They spent the entire night in the church calling upon God for help, kneeling on the floor and raising their hands folded before their mouths. This is the posture in which they were observed by many Indians. Even those who were waking in the middle of the plaza, as well as many Indians who had been allied with the Spaniards since the events of Cajamarca, did the same thing.

The Spaniards' Attack on the Indians in the Fortress of Cuzco

In the early morning of the next day, all the Spaniards left the church and mounted their horses, poised for battle. They looked around and suddenly put their spurs to their horses and, despite their enemies, broke at full speed through the gate, which was sealed like a wall, and made for the hill in the life-and-death flight. When the Indians who were surrounding Cuzco saw them running like this, they cried, "They are fleeing to Castile, they are fleeing to Castile, cut them off. Thus, the entire ring around the city dissolved because some of them were going after them and others tried to cut off the Spaniards' escape route; yet others went to warn those who were guarding the bridge, so that none of them would be able to escape in any direction. When the Spaniards saw themselves pursued by many men, they turned their horses around and went across a mountain called Queancalla in order to attack them from the rear where Vila Oma had taken position. Meanwhile, the latter had climbed up to the fortress of Cuzco, which was called Saczahuaman, in order to take shelter there. The Spaniards fought desperately and took the four gates of the fortress. The Indians hurled many rocks from the mighty walls, shot arrows, and threw lances and spears, which harassed the Spaniards greatly. They killed Juan Pizarro and two blacks as well as many Indians who were allied with the Spaniards. But when Vila Oma's men ran out of ammunition of rocks and other projectiles, the Spaniards, thanks to divine favor,[56] succeeded in penetrating and taking the fortress. Thereby, they killed and crushed many Indians who were inside. Others threw themselves from the walls. The first ones to jump died because the walls were very high; some of those who jumped later survived because they landed on a pile of dead bodies. The battle was very bloody on both sides, because many Indians were fighting for the Spaniards. Among these were two of my father's brothers, Ynguill and Vaipai, as well as many men from his band and Chachapoya and Cañari Indians.

After the fall of the fortress, the battle lasted another three days, for the Indians regrouped on the next day in order to try to retake the fortress. They courageously attacked the Spaniards, who had taken shelter in the fortress; but because of all the guards, consisting of Cañari auxiliary troops as well as Spaniards, they could not harm them. Moreover, these Indians reported the appearance of a white horse, which had been among the first to penetrate the fortress, doing great damage among the Indians.[57] The battle lasted the entire day. At nightfall, the Indians returned to their positions, for they couldn't fight their enemies any longer because of the great darkness. As the Spaniards did not want to give up the fortress, they let them go. The next morning they resumed the battle, which was fought relentlessly on both sides. Finally, when the Indians were attacking the Spaniards with great courage, the Spaniards suddenly broke out of the fortress and launched a fierce counterattack. In the face of this onslaught, the Indians withdrew to Callca, where my father was staying. The Spaniards followed them to the Yucay River, killing or putting to flight a large number of them. There, the Indians eluded the Spaniards, who went on to Callca, where my father was. However, they did not find him there because he was attending a festivity in a town called Sacsasiray. As they could not catch him there, they returned to Cuzco by another way but lost a large amount of their baggage, which the Indians, who had come out of their hiding place, took from their rear guard. Then the Indians, with their booty, made for the village where my father was celebrating.

After the celebrations in the village of Sacsasiray were over, my father went on to the town of Tambo and spent one night in Yucay on the way. When he arrived at Tambo, he had the entire population of the country gather, for he was planning to build a mighty fort in order to defend himself against the Spaniards, who might attack him. After a very short time all were gathered before my father, and he made the following speech:

The Speech that the Inca made to all his Captains in Tambo, whereto he had withdrawn after the failed siege of Cuzco

"My beloved sons and brothers, you know how in my previous speeches I have always kept you from doing harm to those evil people who entered my land under the pretense of being sons of Viracocha and whom I permitted to do so. Because of all the very good things I have done for them and because of giving them everything I had—silver and gold, materials and maize, herds, subjects, women, servants, and countless other things— they took me prisoner. They insulted and maltreated me without reason. Then they tried to kill me, which I found out through Antonico, their translator. He is present here; he ran away from the Spaniards because he couldn't bear it any longer. And as you learned during the mobilization of the troops for the siege of Cuzco, I had withdrawn to Callca so that we could deal them a heavy blow without first making them suspicious. As far as I know, everything has been carried out according to my orders. However, I was not able to be present as I had wanted to. This was detrimental to your effort to conquer the fortress of Saczahuaman, which they took from you because of your negligence. More- over, they then put you to flight, following you to Yucay, without you being able to stop them. It was painful for me to see that you let them get away, despite the fact that you were so numerous and they were but few. Perhaps Viracocha aided them because, as you told me, they worshipped Him all night on their knees. After all, if he didn't help them, what else could explain that they were able to elude you, who were countless in number. But what's done is done. From now on, you must take heed on your life how you deal with them, for you must know that they are our main enemy and that we will always be theirs, because that's the way they have chosen it. I want to take cover in this place and build a fortress that nobody can penetrate. On your life do me this favor, and it may well turn out to be very useful for us one day."

The Chiefs' Response to the Inca

"Sapai Inca, we, who are your humble servants, kiss your hands.[58] We are devastated and embarrassed to come in your sight because of our failure at this most important campaign against these insidious people, who maltreated you so often and repaid your benevolence with such ingratitude. We are thrown into such consternation that we hardly dare to look you in the face but take some consolation in being able to put some of the blame on you. For when we had thoroughly surrounded the enemy and deprived them of all hope for help, we asked you what to do with them and you sent us word that we should let them suffer like they had made you suffer, that you would come and destroy them yourself. In order not to disobey you, we let them be for one day and one night while we were waiting for you. When we were sure of ourselves and deemed them entirely in our hands, they eluded us, and then we were incapable of doing anything to them. We don't know why this happened or what to say about it, except that our misfortune consisted in not striking soon enough and yours in not granting us permission to do so. We are prepared to take upon us the punishment that you want to put on us for our guilt. With regard to your wish to fortify this town so that you may protect yourself from those people and any other possible attackers, we answer that we will gladly comply, for we owe you more than just this." Thus, they turned the town into one of the strongest fortifications in Peru during the year and a half that my father stayed in Tambo.

During this time, after my father had already talked to the Indians and expanded on the misfortune that had come upon them, there arrived in this said town of Tambo some messengers who reported on what had been happening in Lima and Cullcomayo. In Sausa there had been a battle between the Spaniards and the Indians in which the Indians were victorious. They brought my father many heads of Spaniards, as well as two Spaniards who were alive, and one black and four horses. They arrived very happy about their victory, and my father received them with all honors and encouraged the others to fight like them. Just about then, a certain Captain Rodrigo Orgóñez arrived with a group of soldiers in the said town of Tambo in order to fight my father. As soon as my father found out about this, he sent many Indians against the Spaniards so that they would cut off their access to the fortress of Tambo, which is located on the other side of the river. They met each other in a fierce battle on the plain called Pascapampa and Pachar, but neither party could finally claim victory because the Spaniards were much harassed by the cactus plants that grow around there and one of them, as well as three blacks, died in the battle. Another one was captured in the fortress by the Indians because he had gone too far ahead of the others. After the night had parted the battling parties, each retreated into their fortifications. Upon nightfall the Spaniards erected their tents. At dawn they started their fires as though they wanted to continue the battle. However, still before daybreak, they returned to Cuzco. The Indians, who had expected to find them in the morning, found nobody there, which amused them extremely and made them surmise that the Spaniards had fled out of fear. When all this had passed and the Spaniards had returned home, my father, who was still in Tambo, continued with the construction of the fortress. During his stay at Tambo, ten captured and defeated Spaniards who were kept there and were being treated very well, even eating at my father's own table, ran away after receiving a message from Cuzco. However, as they were not very skilled, they were recaptured in a town called Maras, two leagues from Cuzco, and brought back. When my father asked them for the reason why they had run away, they didn't know what to say. One of them was the aforementioned Antonico, who, although he had warned my father against the intrigues of the Spaniards, did not know how to appreciate his good treatment by my father, who had him taken around in his chair and cared for him as though he were his own son. For this reason, he fared the same as the rest of them. They all were ordered to be turned over to some Moyomoyo Indians from the Anti lowlands in order to be hacked to pieces and eaten.

When all of this was over and the construction of the fortress completed, my father announced that he wished to withdraw into the Antian lowlands[59] and to give up the other land, for the Spaniards were harassing him too much and the Anti people were begging him much to settle in their land so that they could protect him and serve him as their king. Being determined to take this step, he had his people summoned in order to explain to them how they were to conduct themselves in living together with the Spaniards.

Manco Inca's Instructions[60] to the Indians about how to conduct themselves toward the Spaniards when he decided to withdraw to the Anti

"My beloved sons and brothers, all of you who are present here and who have accompanied me in my trials and tribulations will hardly guess, I suppose, why I have summoned you now. But I will explain it to you presently. On your life, don't let the things I have to say disturb you, for you know that necessity often compels people to do things that they don't want to do. For this reason, I can't help but acquiesce to those Anti Indians, who have been begging me for some time to visit them. I will do them this favor and stay with them for a few days. I ask you that you please not be upset, because I do not want to cause you any pain, for I love you like my own children. I would be very happy if you carried out this wish.

"You are well aware, and I have often told you before, how these bearded men intruded into my land under the pretense of being Viracochas. Considering their clothes and other characteristics that are entirely different from our own, this did not seem implausible to you and even to me. Because of this and also because of the reports of the Tallana Yunca people, who observed them doing certain things in their country, I permitted them, as you know, to come into my country and into my cities. I treated them in the way that is well-known throughout the entire land. As you know, I gave them many things, after which—and because of which—they treated me in the manner that you have witnessed. Not only they but also my brothers Pascac, Ynguill, and Huaipar deprived me of my land and even made an attempt on my life. However, I eluded this attempt thanks to Antonico's warning, as I have told you the other day in this place. He was eaten by the Anti people because he did not know how to behave. In the face of all of these and many other things, which I will omit here in order to avoid prolixity, I have summoned you to Cuzco in order to pay them back for a small part of all of that which they have done to us. But your design did not succeed because, I think, they were aided by their god or because I wasn't present. This gave me great pains, but we shouldn't wonder or agonize about it too much, for not all of men's designs always work out the way we would like it. Therefore, I appeal to you not to despair; after all, things could have been worse, considering that we also caused them some damage. Thus, as you know, we captured a few of them in Lima, in Cullcomayo, and in Jauja, which might bring us some consolation, even though it doesn't measure up to the pains they have given us.

"It seems to me that the time has come for me to depart for the land of the Antis, as I told you earlier. I will have to remain there for several days. Keep in mind my command not to forget what I have told you and what I am still about to tell you now, which is the following: keep in mind how long my grandfathers and great-grandfathers, and I as well, have sustained and protected you, and how we have furthered and governed your households, providing for them according to your needs. Therefore, you and your descendants are obliged never to forget me, my grandfathers, and great-grandfathers for your entire lives, but to respect and obey my son and brother Titu Cusi Yupanqui and my other sons and their descendents. By doing so, you will give me great joy; and they will thank you according to the instructions with which I leave them. May these words be enough for you now."

The Indians' Answer to the Inca

"Sapai Inca, how can you leave your sons behind with such a heavy heart? They have desired nothing but to serve you and would even risk their lives for you a thousand times if necessary! To the care of which king, which master, are you leaving them? What disservice, what betrayal, what evil deed have we done to you that you want to abandon us like this, helpless and without a master or king to respect? Never have we known another master or father but you, your father Huayna Capac, and his ancestors. Don't leave us like this, master, without protection and consolation but grant us, if you will, the joy of accompanying you to wherever it is that you want to go. All of us, children and adults, men and women, are ready to follow you and don't want to abandon you, even though you may leave us." When my father saw how anxious all of his people were to serve him, he gave them the following answer:

"I thank you, my sons, for the willingness and desire that you have shown for following me to wherever I need to go. You will not have to regret your investment in me, for you will receive my gratitude and compensation sooner than you might think. But now, on your life, be composed and don't anguish so much, for I will see you again very soon. From now until I return or until I send word through a messenger, you shall do the following, which shall be your way of life. First, you are not to believe anything that these bearded ones, who have mocked me because of my good faith, may say for they lie a lot, as they have lied to me in all their dealings with me, and they will continue to lie in their dealings with you as well. One thing you could do is to pretend on the outside that you agree to their demands and to give them a small trinket now and then, depending on what your land yields. These people are so crude and so different from us that they may take from you by force what you don't give them; and they may abuse you because of it. The best way to prevent this from happening is to act exactly as I tell you. Second, you are to keep yourself ready for the time when I send for you or when I send word about what is to be done with these people. In the case that they attack you or try to take your land from you, always defend yourself, even though you might lose your life in the attempt. If you are in extreme difficulty and need my personal presence, send word through messengers, regardless of where I might be. And watch yourself, for they deceive with their pretty words and later keep nothing that they have said. For this is the way they conducted themselves toward me, as you have seen, when they told me that they were sons of the god Viracocha and initially showed me great friendship and love but later treated me in the way you have seen. If they had been the sons of Viracocha as they claimed to be, they wouldn't have done what they have done. For Viracocha can change the mountains into a plain, make the rivers run dry, and raise mountains where there have been none before, but he never hurts anyone. We have seen nothing of this in their behavior. On the contrary, instead of doing good things, they have done bad things to us by violently and deceitfully depriving us of our possessions, wives, sons, daughters, fields, food, and many other things that we had in our country—all against our will. We can hardly consider people who act like this to be sons of Viracocha; but rather, as I have said on other occasions, sons of *supai,* or worse, for they have imitated him in their actions and did things too depraved for me to mention.

Further, they may order you to worship what they themselves worship, namely some sort of painted rags that they claim to be Viracocha. Even though they are just mere rags, they will demand that you pray to these rags as you would pray to our huacas.[61] Don't do it but keep with what we have, for, as you can see, the *villcas*[62] speak to us; we can see the sun and the moon with our own eyes, but we can't see whatever it is that they are talking about. Now and then, I suppose, they will get you to worship what they worship through force and deceit. By all means, go through with it while they are present if you can't help it. But never forget our own ceremonies. If they were to order you to bring forth your huacas in order to have them destroyed, show them only what you have to but hide the rest. This way you will make me very happy."

After all of these and many other things, my father said farewell to the Indians and on this occasion put me in front of them, saying that I was his son and that they would have to regard me as their master after his death. Then, when he rose to his feet, all broke into such loud cries that one had the impression that they would pierce the mountains. In their anxiety the people wanted to follow him, but my father would not allow it except in those cases where absolutely nothing could hold them back. He asked those who wanted to follow him with such persistence how they could leave their fields, their houses, their wives, and children, as well as their *uyawas*, or animals, in order to follow him.[63] He told them to control themselves and that he would come to visit them very soon or send word about what they were to do. Thus, he departed from all of them for the town of Vitcos.

The Inca's Arrival at Vitcos

After our arrival at Vitcos, a town thirty leagues away from Cuzco, we and the people who had accompanied my father took a break with the intention of staying and resting there for a few days. My father had a house built for his sleeping quarters, for the houses that were already there belonged to my ancestors Pachacuti Inca, Topa Inca Yupanqui, Huayna Capac, and others, whose bodies we had put there,[64] because we didn't dare to leave them in Cuzco or in Tambo. A little while later, when my father had regained his calm and composure and was no longer suspicious that somebody might intrude into this country, he followed the invitation of the Anti and the other peoples of this country and wanted to hold a very solemn celebration. When the celebration had reached its climax, they suddenly, and without comprehending what was happening, saw themselves surrounded by Spaniards. Because the Indians were feeling very heavy with drink and had left their weapons at home, they were surprised and unable to defend themselves against Don Diego de Almagro, the Captain Diego Ordoñez,[65] Gonzalo Pizarro, and the many others, who are too many to enumerate here. They took as many Indians, men and women, as they could, as well as the mummies of my ancestors, whose names were the following: Vanacauri, Viracocha Inca, Pachacuti Inca, Topa Inca Yupanqui, and Huayna Capac, as well as many mummies of women and jewelry and ornaments, which were being displayed during this festivity. Also, fifty thousand head of choice livestock, the best that was to be had in that country, from the estate of my ancestors and my father. Also, they kidnapped as well several coyas. My father and several others barely eluded them, and the Spaniards returned very contented with their booty, and me, to Cuzco.[66] After our arrival at Cuzco, a so-and-so Oñate took me into his house, where he treated me very well and took care of me.[67] When my father found out about this, he sent a messenger to Oñate in order to thank him and to officially put me and my two sisters into his care, asking him to look after me and them and promising that he would show his gratitude. During the time after the celebration while I was staying with the said Oñate, my father left Vitcos because some generals from the Chachapoya people had offered to accompany him to a city called Rabanto,[68] for there was a good fortress where they could defend themselves against all their enemies. After thinking about their offer, he accepted it. On the way to Rabanto he rested a few days in a town called Oroncoy, because the inhabitants wanted to hold a celebration in his honor. While he was still there, he sent scouts in order to find out whether there were any Spaniards or other people who might stand in his way in the area. It is reported that after he had sent them, around dawn more than two hundred heavily armed Spaniards appeared on horse in the village of Oroncoy in search of my father. They had captured the guards on the bridges that were there and had tortured them with ropes in order to extort information about the whereabouts of my father. They [the guards] told them that he was at the village called Oroncoy. The Spaniards left the guards behind and galloped at full speed, one behind the other, up the hill in the hope that they would catch my father in his sleep or at least before he was able to make preparations for his defense. But my aunt Cura Oclo, my father's sister, spotted the approaching troops from afar after hearing the thumping noises of the horses. With great alarm, she rushed into my father's sleeping quarters in order to warn him that the enemies were approaching and to tell him to rise and attack them. When my father saw her so terrified, he rose in a hurry without taking care of anything else in order to find out if what his sister was saying was true. From his elevated point of view, he could immediately see that she was right. He hurried back to his house and ordered the bit to be put on his horse, for he wanted to gather his people immediately and just as he was, so that the enemies would not fall upon them before they were ready to fight. As soon as his horse was for ready for battle, he had it saddled, for his enemies were already close.[69] He positioned a great number of women on top of the hill, all armed with lances in order to evoke the impression that they were men. After that, he swiftly jumped on his horse, his lance in hand. He shielded all of his men all by himself, so that the enemies would not be able to hurt them as long as the scouts, who were surveying the country, had not returned. They [the scouts] arrived on top of the hill almost at the same time as the Spaniards, while my father was fighting them off by himself. When they arrived there, they were exhausted by their ascent. But when they saw my father fight so bravely, they found new encouragement to fight their enemies, who were still farther downhill. They courageously fell upon them in a throng with their lances and shields and pushed them down the hill. After they had dealt them this blow, they took a rest in order to catch their breath. When the Spaniards noticed that they had sat down to take a drink, they assumed that they were exhausted and boldly resumed their attack up the hill. Our men, however, had been on the watch and had reinforced themselves with people who had come to their aid from various places. As soon as they saw their enemies approach with such resolve, they fell upon them and drove them apart in one blow, throwing them over the cliffs and rocks into the abyss. The helpless Spaniards had been so exhausted from the weight of their armor and from the heat, that they weren't able to resist and to avert their collective destruction. Not a single horse nor man escaped with his life, except for two men: one by swimming across the river and the other by grabbing hold of one of the ropes of the bridge.

Thus, after their victory had been completed, my father's men went about collecting the spoils from the Spaniards and stripped every one of them that they could get their hands on, taking their clothes and weapons and bringing everything up into the village of Oroncoy. My father and his people were very much elated by the victory that they had accomplished and made a celebration and dance that lasted for five days in order to honor the spoils and the victory. After this celebration, and after all of these things had happened, my father set out with all of his people for a several days' march to the town of Rauantu, which is located in the direction of Quito. As he was crossing the valley of Jauja, in a town called Llacjapalanga he learned that the natives of this land, the Guanca people, had allied themselves with the Spaniards.[70] He was very much enraged by this and decided to punish them in a way that would set an example for the entire country. He made it known that, because they had obeyed and submitted to the Spaniards, he would burn them and their houses without permitting anyone to be spared, including their women, daughters, and sons who served a powerful huaca called Guari Villca, whom they worshipped in a certain valley about five leagues from Xaxallaga.

When the Guanca people found out that my father was angry with them and intended to burn them and their idol Guari Villca on account of them having allied themselves with the Spaniards in spite of the fact he [Manco Inca] was their legitimate ruler, they decided to prevent his entry by sending word to the Spaniards and by putting themselves under their protection in order to extricate themselves from their precarious situation. As soon as the Spaniards heard about my father's decision to destroy the Guancas, a hundred of them rushed to their defense.

When my father found out about this, he changed his course and fought many battles against the Guancas in several places, spreading death and destruction and calling out, "May your masters help you now!" Thus, after a march that lasted several days, he arrived at a place called Jauja la Grande. There he was engaged in a bigger battle with the Spaniards and the Guancas that lasted two days. Finally, my father emerged victorious, thanks to the large number of people and to his skill. They killed fifty Spaniards and put the others to flight in full gallop. Some of our men went after them for awhile, but when they saw how fast they were running away, they returned to my father, who was swinging his lance high on his horse on which he had fought the Spaniards so valiantly. After the battle had ended, my father, somewhat tired from the fighting, descended from his horse and sat down to rest with his people, who were all very exhausted from the battle and many of them injured. The next day, when the people were somewhat refreshed, they took a break from all the marching at a town called Vayocache,[71] which is not far from the place of the idol called Guari Villca. While he was staying there, my father ordered the idol to be excavated from where it had been buried up to the shoulders. After it had been excavated on all sides, he had the entire treasure that had been placed there as an offering brought before him, as well as the *yanaconas*, the male and female servants,[72] who had been left in charge of the keeping of this idol, in which the inhabitants of this country had much faith. Then he ordered all of them killed in order to demonstrate that he alone was the ruler. Also, they placed a rope around the idol's neck and dragged it for the entire journey of twenty leagues over hills and rocks, swamps and mud, heaping great insults upon it and saying, "Just think about the faith that those Guancas placed in this idol, even believing it to be Viracocha, and now look how it's ended up, as well as their masters, the Spaniards." As they were thus proceeding with their journey, they arrived at a town called Acostambo,[73] where they stayed for one year. There they built houses and cultivated fields, which are now owned by Spaniards and are now called Viñaca, for there is much Castilian wine to be seen there. The huaca, or idol, called Guari Villca was, upon order of my father, thrown into a large river.[74]

After this, my father went to a region and town called Pillcorumi.[75] He went there upon the request of some Anti leaders, who kept begging him to come. There he was once more engaged in battle by a group of Spaniards who had come in search of him; but he beat and dispersed them. It would lead too far astray here if I were to recount all the details; suffice it to note that in the process a great amount of artillery, harquebuses, lances, crossbows, and other weapons fell into his hands. After he had fought another battle with the Spaniards at Yeñupay, he stayed there for another year. Thereafter, he returned to Vitcos, and from there made his way back to Vilcabamba, stopping on the way in several towns that I will omit here for brevity's sake. Having arrived, he rested and recovered for a few days and built his houses and lodgings in order to settle down there, for it seemed to him like a good site for his capital seat.

After a few days of rest, when he was just starting to think that the Spaniards would leave him alone, he had word from the scouts whom he had positioned along the way that Gonzalo Pizarro and Captain Diego Maldonado and Ordónez,[76] as well as many others, were approaching and that they were accompanied by his three brothers, who were Don Pablo,[77] Ynguill, and Huaspar. The Spaniards made them go first, for they maintained that they intended to ally themselves with my father against the Spaniards. My father went out in order to intercept them at a fortress that he had in his control about three leagues away. He intended to defend himself against them there and not to let them take this bastion. When he arrived there, he faced a great number of Spaniards. (I am not sure how many exactly, as they were difficult to count because of the dense forest.) They battled each other fiercely from the opposite banks of a river—the one on one side and the other on the other side. After ten days, the battle still had not ended, for the Spaniards fought in shifts against my father's hordes and against him. But they fared poorly throughout because we held the fortress. The situation became even more precarious when a brother of my aunt Cura Oclo by the name of Huaipar turned up there. This would later cost him his life, for my father was extremely enraged that he had dared to go against him. When my father, beside himself with rage, wanted to kill him, Cura Oclo tried to prevent him from it, because she loved him [Huaipar] very much. But my father was not inclined to grant her request and beheaded him and his other brother Ynguill, exclaiming, "It is more just that their heads be cut off than to let them take mine." My aunt, who was very upset about the death of her brother, did not ever want to move from the spot where their bodies were laid.

In the midst of these events, still before they were completely over, a few Spaniards came to the place where my father was. When he saw them approach and realized that there was no escape, he decided to jump into the water and to swim across the river. Having arrived on the opposite bank, he exclaimed loudly, "I am Manco Inca, I am Manco Inca!" When the Spaniards realized that they would not be able to catch him, they decided to return to Cuzco and drove before them Cura Oclo and Cusi Rimache, another one of my father's brothers whom he had with him, among other things. They arrived with my aunt at the town of Pampaconac, where they tried to rape her. But she did not want to let this happen and defended herself bravely to the bitter end, even covering her body with stinking and filthy things in order to disgust those who wanted to touch her. Thusly she defended herself innumerable times until they arrived at the town of Tambo, where the Spaniards, who were very angry because my aunt would not permit what they desired and because she was my father's sister, shot her with arrows. For the sake of chastity, she endured it all and, while the others shot arrows at her, exclaimed, "Will you take revenge on a woman for your annoyance? What would another woman do in my place? Hurry up and kill me, so that your appetite may be satisfied!" Thus, they murdered her while she covered her eyes with a piece of cloth.

When Vila Oma, my father's former commanding general, as well as Ticoc, Taipi, Tanquihualpa, Orco Varanca, Atoc Suyru, and many other former generals of my father saw that the Spaniards had captured and abused the coya in this manner,[78] they were very upset. This was not lost on the Spaniards, who took them and said, "Surely, you will revert to your old love of the Inca and ally yourself with him. But we won't let it happen, for you will die here along with your mistress." They defended themselves against these accusations and said that they did not intend to do this, that they wanted to stay with the Spaniards and serve them. The Spaniards, however, who did not believe them and thought that their protestations were feigned, had them all burnt to death. After they had been burnt and the coya killed, they went on to Yucay, where they burned Ozcollo, Coriatao, and many others in order to prevent them from joining my father and in order to cover their backs. After all these things related here had passed and many more that I have omitted for brevity's sake, my father returned to Vilcabamba, the capital of this province, and lived there in peace for a few days. Because he missed me, he sent me several messengers from that town to Cuzco, where I had been staying since my abduction from Vitcos at the house of the aforementioned Oñate. The messengers, however, abducted me and my mother and secretly brought us from Cuzco to the town of Vitcos, where my father was staying in order to refresh himself, for it was located in a cool region. There my father and I spent many days. During this time, seven Spaniards appeared there, each of whom arrived on a different day. They claimed that they were on the run for some crimes they had committed, and they protested their willingness to serve my father to the best of their abilities for the duration of their entire lives.[79] They begged for permission to stay in his land for the remainder of their days. Although my father would hardly have been prejudiced in favor of the Spaniards by then, when he saw that they had come with good intentions, he ordered his captains not to harm them, for he wanted to protect them in his land as though they were his own offspring. They were even to be given houses in which they could live. Although my father's captains would have preferred to finish them off then and there, they obeyed his orders. My father hosted them for days, even years, treating them very well and supplying them with everything they needed. He even ordered his own women to prepare food and drink for them. Not enough, he had them accompany him, treating them and enjoying himself with them as though they were his brothers.

After some days and years while the said Spaniards were in my father's company in his own house in Vitcos, my father, they, and I were enjoying ourselves by playing a game of *herrón*.[80] My father, being unsuspecting, gave no credit to an Indian woman who was in the service of one of the Spaniards named Barba and who had reported a few days earlier that the Spaniards wanted to kill him. But my father, without suspecting anything in this or any other regard, was enjoying himself with them as he had before. When, in the course of the game, my father went to pick up the iron with which they were playing, they all fell upon him with daggers, knives, and some swords. Feeling his injuries, my father attempted to defend himself on all sides, invigorated by the fury with which approaching death inspired him. He being alone, however, and there being seven of them and because he did not have any weapons, they threw his wounded body to the ground several times and left him there for dead. When I, still being very young, saw them treat my father this way, I tried to rush to his aid, but they angrily turned on me and threw at me my father's personal lance, which happened to be there, thus almost killing me as well. Frightened and terrified by this, I ran down some wooded slopes, so that they wouldn't find me if they came after me. They left my father, who was on his last gasps, and went out the door in good spirits, saying, "Don't worry; we've already killed the Inca." But several Antis, who were just arriving, as well as the Captain Rimache Yupanqui, surrounded them and, before they could get away, cut off their escape route, threw them off their horses, and dragged them away in order to sacrifice them. They killed all of them in a cruel manner, even burning some of them alive. Before my father died,[81] he summoned all of his captains, as well as me, in order to talk to us. He addressed his captains with the following words.

The Inca's Dying Speech to his Captains

He said, "My sons, here you see how I fared because I was too trusting toward these Spanish people, especially those seven whom you have gotten to know here. I treated them like sons, and after I had protected them for such a long time, they have reciprocated my hospitality in this manner. I don't believe I will emerge from this alive. But, on your lives, remember how I have warned you again and again—in Cuzco, in Tambo, and in all the other towns where you gathered following my call, as well as in the places to which you have followed me. Because I know well that you have committed all of this to your memory, I don't want to reiterate it. Neither do my pains permit it, nor is there any reason to torture you even more with it. I leave my son Titu Cusi Yupanqui in your care. Look after him, for you know that he is the apple of my eye and that I used to treat him more like a brother than a son, owing to his intelligence. I have also instructed him to take care of all of you and all my children, to look after them as I would have done. I ask that you treat him like you treated me; and I am convinced that he will appreciate it very much and repay you accordingly. Therefore, call him, so I can give him my blessings and tell him what to do."

Manco Inca's Dying Speech to his Son

"My beloved son, you can see well what's happening to me, so I don't need to express in words my pain, which is obvious in the facts. Do not weep, for if there is anyone who has reason to weep, it is me, provided I still could. For I have myself brought about this situation in which I now find myself by trusting people of that sort and by spoiling those who did not deserve it. As you know, they came here on the run from their comrades because of certain crimes they had committed. I took them in and favored them with paternal sympathy. But listen to what I have to say: I order you never to deal with people like these, so you won't end up like me. Don't allow them to enter into your lands, regardless of how much they try to persuade you with words. I was fooled by their sickly sweet words; and the same will happen to you if you trust them.

I entrust to you your brothers and sisters, as well as your mother. Look after them, help and support them, as I have done for you. Look out so that you don't dishonor my bones by mal-treating your siblings and your mother, for you know that this would hurt me very much. I also entrust these poor Indians to you. Take care of them as you are supposed to and remember how they gave up their lands and their homes out of love for me and how they have accompanied, guarded, and protected me in the course of all my trials. Don't work them too hard and don't harass them; don't scold or punish them without cause, for this would bring forth the wrath of Viracocha. I have ordered them to respect and revere you in my place as their ruler, for you are my firstborn son and the heir of my kingdom. This is my last will.[82] I trust in their benevolence and know that they will accept and respect you. They will do nothing but what I have told them to do and what you will order them to do."

After these words, he expired and left me in the town of Vitcos. From there I moved to Vilcabamba, where I remained for more than twenty years until some Indians from Huamachuco disturbed my peace. They had been sent by the court of justice at Cuzco on orders of Gonzalo Pizarro, who was then rebelling against the king.

How I, Don Diego de Castro Titu Cusi Yupanqui, made peace with the Spaniards and subsequently became a Christian, thanks to God, whom we used to call Viracocha

Above I have explained briefly and succinctly why my father Manco Inca Yupanqui was the natural ruler of these kingdoms of Peru, the manner in which the Spaniards intruded into his country, and how and why he resisted them—the reason being their many abuses—as well as the course and end of his life. Here I want to relate how I've fared since his days and of the manner in which I've converted to Christianity and made peace with the Spaniards. It was a blessing of God that the governor licentiate Don Lope García de Castro then ruled and administered these kingdoms of Peru. This is how it happened.

At the time when the Marquis de Cañete was the viceroy of these kingdoms of Peru,[83] he sent me a padre from the Dominican order in this land where I live in order to negotiate with me about my removal to Cuzco. The padre announced that the viceroy had orders from the emperor Don Carlos that obligated him to treat me according to my rank if I were to leave my land and convert to Christianity. But then I remembered the treatment that the Spaniards had accorded to my father when they were in Cuzco with him, as well as the orders that he had given us upon his death and I thought that the same could happen to me. For this reason, I did not want to consent to the proposal that the padre, a certain brother Melchor de los Reyes, who had been sent in this matter, and his companion, a certain Juan Sierra, conveyed on behalf of the viceroy. But in order to see whether what the padre and his companion said was true, I sent a few of my captains along with the said padre to the marquis, so that they could clarify this matter. I conveyed my intention that I would send one of my brothers in my place if what they were saying was true. He would be able to test the Spaniards' way of life and report to me how they were conducting themselves toward him. If their conduct was good, I would follow later.

A year later, the said padre and my captains returned and confirmed everything. When I saw that such a person [as important as the marquis] was begging me so insistently and gave me such credible confirmation that my needs would be taken care of, I sent my brother Saire Topa, after having instructed him on how to conduct himself. As soon as this was done, he went with the said padre to the viceroy, who assigned to him the valley of Yucay and other tracts [repartimientos] for his sustenance, where he died a Christian.[84] When I learned of his death, I was very upset, for I thought that the Spaniards had murdered him as they had already murdered my father. I spent several days worrying about this until they sent me the licentiate Polo with Martín de Pando, who has stood by my side as my notary to this day, and Juan de Betanzos from Cuzco with the news that my brother Saire Topa had died a natural death. After I had acknowledged this news, I kept Martín de Pando in my land and let Juan de Betanzos return with my answer.[85] I stayed there for several days until I had another visit from several messengers who had been sent on behalf of the Count of Nieva, who had succeeded the Marquis de Cañete as viceroy, with a proposal for peace. This proposal was the same as the one the marquis had sent, and I answered that I was ready to make peace if they returned some of the lands of my father that the king had appropriated. Thus, the messengers went off with this answer.

I think that the Spaniards' efforts for peace had one of three possible causes: because they knew that I continuously made raiding expeditions into their lands and abducted a great number of the inhabitants; or because the king had ordered what his conscience told him to do, considering what he had obtained from my father; or perhaps because they wanted to have me close by them in their land in order to make sure that I wouldn't cause them any more harm. As I was not indoctrinated with regard to matters concerning the faith, it did not occur to me then as it does to me now that the most important reason may have been their desire to convert me to Christianity. Only now, after the fathers have explained it to me, do I understand that this was one of the reasons and the most important one.

After the said messengers who had come on behalf of the Count of Nieva had left, the treasurer García de Melo came with the same request. He asked me to discontinue hostilities and to refrain from raiding expeditions so that the Spaniards may have peace, saying that the king would compensate me if I allowed missionaries to come to my land in order to preach the word of God. I answered his request—which was to discontinue hostilities, not to harm the Indians, and not to harass the Spaniards—by promising to keep the peace unless they gave me reason to do otherwise and that the proof of it would be in the facts. With regard to his request to allow priests into my land, I answered that I knew nothing of that business, that the first thing was to make peace and that thereafter one could still do what seemed right. This was the answer with which the treasurer Melo left the first time.[86]

At the time when this back and forth between Cuzco and my land was going on, a certain doctor by the name of Cuenca, His Majesty's auditor [oidor], was the royally appointed judge [corregidor] of Cuzco. One day a group of Indians, who had been assigned to Nuño de Mendoza and who lived on the banks of a river called Acobamba, ran away because of the abuses to which the Spanish overseer had subjected them. They crossed the border into my land in order to pay tribute to me as their master. When the doctor Cuenca heard of this, he thought that I had forcefully abducted the Indians and wrote me a very rude letter in which he demanded that I return the Indians to their master or else he would wage a war on me more savage than any that had ever been seen. When I saw this letter, I was very upset and responded that I was innocent of the things of which I was accused but that I was always ready for war any time they might come, if that's what they wanted. In my anger, I prepared my people for this possibility and ordered that scouts be positioned all over the place, so that those who wished me evil would not be able to approach unnoticed. The said doctor Cuenca never responded to me in this matter, so I went to the road that he would have to take in order to find out whether he was intent on going through with the campaign he had announced. I brought more than five hundred Indians from various places back from this expedition and returned calmly home. Having arrived there, I received a letter from the said doctor Cuenca. It had been written in Lima but I don't know how it reached me. In it, he offered his services and asked me to let bygones be bygones.

Thereafter, the treasurer García de Melo appeared once again with a dispatch from Your Excellency.[87] He counseled me to go ahead with what I had already proposed to him, which was to marry my son Don Felipe Quispe Titu with his cousin Doña Beatriz. Thus, we came to an agreement on how to make peace, and later he and I sealed it in Acobamba with Your Majesty's mandate.[88] As witnesses of this event, we brought His Majestry's appointees Diego Rodríguez as judge [corregidor] and Martín de Pando as secretary. As Your Excellency is in possession of an extensive account of this and can present it to His Majesty, I will not mention here any details about the manner in which this agreement and treaty came about or about anything else.

After all, Your Excellency is Yourself the author of this arrangement—beginning with the meeting at Chuquichaca and the arrival of Hernando Matienzo up to my conversion and baptism.
But I wanted to make sure that His Majesty will learn from me
personally that Your Excellency has been the principal cause of
this.

When Your Excellency sent me Diego Rodríguez in order to
serve as the corregidor in my land, I accepted him, as you know,
because he had been sent by Your Excellency and because I realized that this was necessary in order to accomplish peace. After
all, I had committed myself to this peace with the king, our lord,
and his vassals. I have kept the peace in every respect. First, I
have received the auditor [oidor] and licentiate Matienzo at the
Chuquichaca bridge and gave him information about certain
things that were happening in my country; second, I permitted
priests to come into my country so that they could instruct me
and my people in things relating to God, as for example in the
case of the padre Vera,[89] who had been sent by Your Excellency.
He baptized my son Don Felipe Quispe Titu and stayed in my
land for almost a year and a half before leaving it upon the arrival of the Augustinian monks, who came to baptize me.

He can also give testimony with regard to this peace and
confirm everything relating to the renunciation that I made to
Your Excellency in the name of His Majesty about all of my kingdoms and possessions, not more or less than my father used to
own. So much was concluded by the treasurer Melo in Acobamba
but all of which I omit here since Your Excellency is a witness
and main actor in these affairs. Moreover, this is the manner in
which I have hitherto kept—and am still keeping—the Christian
faith. As Your Excellency has asked me in so many letters to
become a Christian because it would be beneficial for maintain-
ing the peace, I attempted to get information from Diego
Rodríguez and Martín de Pando about who among the monks in
Cuzco was the most outstanding personality and which religion

enjoyed the widest approbation and power. They explained to me that the mightiest, most respected, and most flourishing religion was that of the Lord St. Augustine and his prior. In other words, the prior of the monks of this particular order residing in Cuzco had the most outstanding personality among all the monks of Cuzco. As I heard and understood this to be so, I became more attached to this order and religion than to any other and decided to write a number of letters to this prior asking him to come personally in order to baptize me, for I preferred him to any other for my baptism, given that he was such an outstanding personality. He, being a very honorable monk, did me the favor of coming into my country in order to baptize me. He also brought another monk, as well as Gonzalo Pérez de Vivero and Tilano de Anaya.[90] They arrived in the town of Rayangalla on 12 August 1568. I came there from Vilcabamba in order to be baptized, for I assumed that this was the reason why they had come. The said prior, fray Juan de Vivero,[91] his companion, and the others remained in that town of Rayangalla for fourteen days in order to instruct me in the matters of faith. Thereafter, on the day of the glorious doctor St. Augustine, the said prior baptized me. Gonzalo Pérez de Vivero was my godfather and Doña Angelina Sisa Ocllo my godmother. After the baptism, the said prior remained there for eight more days in order to strengthen my knowledge in all the things relating to our Holy Catholic faith and to teach me about its things and mysteries. After all of this had been done, the said prior departed with Gonzalo Pérez de Vivero and left me in the care of one of his companions by the name of fray Marcos García, who was supposed to give me further guidance on the things that the prior had taught me and to preach and teach the word of God also to my people.[92] Before they left, however, I explained to my Indians the reasons why I had let myself be baptized and why I had called these people into my country, as well as the benefits that people derived from baptism and why the said padre had remained in our land. They all responded that they were glad that I had been baptized and that the padre would remain in our land, saying that they would soon follow to do the same, since that was the reason for which the padre was in our land.

Two months after the prior had departed, the said padre in Rayangalla had begun to teach the faith and had already baptized a few infants with the permission of their parents. Then he decided to visit the land beyond the mountain passages of Huamanga with Martín de Pando. He remained there for a period of four months, performing the same services and putting up crosses and churches. He passed through eight towns, building churches in three of them and erecting crosses in the rest. All together, he baptized ninety infants. After he had finished with that and had left boys there who were to teach the Word, he returned to the said town of Rayangalla, where he remained alone for seven months in order to baptize and instruct the Indians. In the month of September,[93] he was joined by another padre. They both lived in that part of the country until I had them come to Vilcabamba, which is where we currently are. Here they haven't baptized anyone yet, for the people here are still too inexperienced in the things that they have to learn about God's law and commandments. I will see to it that they will learn those things in due time. I have tried to convey to Your Excellency in the manner mentioned above — that is, summarily and without further details — the course and manner of my father's life, as well as the outcome of my negotiations up to the present point in time, so that Your Excellency can convey everything to His Majesty. Your Excellency can let me know if there is a need for more detail here or there about things as they have happened and are happening now, and your wish will be my command. In the meantime, I trust that this will suffice, although more things could certainly be noted and said according to our ways of expression, especially with regard to our origins and beginnings, about our dress, and the manner of our people. However, in order to avoid prolixity, I will omit these things here, for they add nothing to the subject matter with which we are concerned here. This leaves me with only one more request, after Your Excellency has already favored me in so many things: that you may explain everything that is written here to His Majesty truthfully and enthusiastically. Hereby, you would do me a great favor, for I hope that His Majesty will, as my master, always favor me. With this I end, for I think that I have gone on enough.

The foregoing account was based on the testimony given by the illustrious Don Titu Cusi Yupanqui, son of Manco Inca, formerly the legitimate ruler of these kingdoms of Peru. It was redacted[94] and arranged by the reverend padre fray Marcos García, monk and priest of the Order of St. Augustine, who was stationed in this province of Vilcabamba with the assignment to minister to the souls that live there for the honor and glory of the Almighty — Father, Son, and Holy Spirit, three entities in one single, true God — and of the glorious Queen of Angels, the Mother of God, Holy Mary, our mistress, now and forever. Amen.

I, Martín de Pando, notary in the service of the illustrious licentiate Don Lope García de Castro, formerly governor of these kingdoms, confirm that all of the foregoing account was dictated and arranged by the said padre upon the insistence of the said Don Diego de Castro. I wrote it down with my own hand, exactly as the padre dictated it to me. The reverend fray Diego Ortiz, priest of the said order who lived together with the author of this account, as well as three captains of the said Don Diego de Castro, namely Suya Yupanqui, Rimache Yupanqui, and Sullca Varac, were eyewitnesses to the transcription and dictation of the account. I notarize the foregoing with my signature. Finished in San Salvador de Vilcabamba, this sixth day of the month of February, in the year 1570. Further notarization is given by the signatures of the said padre, fray Marcos García and fray Diego Ortiz, as well as myself, said Martín de Pando. I, fray Marcos García, confirm having been present during the dictation, as witnessed by fray Diego Ortiz and verified by Martín de Pando, notary.

I, Don Diego de Castro Titu Cusi Yupanqui, son of Manco Inca Yupanqui, formerly legitimate ruler of this kingdom of Peru, affirm that I—because it was necessary for me to give an account to our lord, King Don Philip, about the things that concern me and my descendants but since I am unfamiliar with the phrases and modes of expression used by the Spaniards in such writings—have asked the reverend fray Don Marcos García and the secretary Martín de Pando to arrange and compose the said account in their customary ways of expression so that it be sent to the illustrious licentiate Don Lope García de Castro in the kingdoms of Spain and with my explicit authorization be presented and related to His Majesty, our lord and king Don Philip. May His Majesty honor me, my sons, and descendants with royal favors commensurate with my rights to compensation. I composed this note for the purpose of verifying the foregoing words and signed it with my name. Finished on the above-mentioned day, month, and year. Don Diego de Castro Titu Cusi Yupanqui.

Power of Attorney for the Governor, licentiate Don Lope García de Castro

Whoever may see this authorization may be informed that I, Sapai Inca Don Diego de Castro Titu Cusi Yupanqui, legitimate son and heir and grandson of Manco Inca Yupanqui and Huayna Capac, formerly the legitimate rulers of these kingdoms and provinces of Peru, declare the following. As I necessarily have many dealings in the kingdoms of Spain with our lord, King Don Philip, with other authorities of various rank and nature, both secular and ecclesiastic, as well as with certain other persons who have removed from these kingdoms to those of Spain and have perhaps even settled there; and as it would be impossible to find anyone who would attend to my affairs with greater diligence and sympathy than the lord governor, the *licenciado* Castro, who is in the process of departing for the kingdom of Spain, or anyone who would take them more to his heart than he has always done and is still doing; and as I therefore trust him entirely, I hereby give him sufficient, absolute, and appropriately legitimate power of attorney as I myself possess and as it is required by law in such cases. I empower him to appear on my behalf and in my name before His Majesty and to present to His Majesty any petition or any petitions and to testify and bear witness on anything he may be asked about relating to my affairs; to appear before any judge, court [*audiencias*], mayor, and office and before any of His Majesty's authorities, ecclesiastical and secular; to petition for every- and anything that in his judgment may or should be due to me; to demand and claim; to protect and defend; to possess, manage, and dispose of these things, as I would possess, manage, and dispose of them personally; and to send everything that is to be had in this manner in the way of gold or silver pesos, goods, interest, herds, or other things to me in this kingdom at my expense. I further empower him to acquire in my name and on my behalf, and with an unspecified amount of my gold pesos, things, estates, or goods that, in his best judgment, seem appropriate for me, whether it be moveable or fixed assets. He also has the power to file any petitions or requests; to take oaths of libel or procedure; to say the truth; to take counteraction to the actions of an opposing party; to make comparisons; to present and withdraw witnesses, scriptural evidence, diplomas, permissions, royal edicts and any other sort of evidence; to contradict an opposing party; to declare any rejection, suspicion, and objection; to swear upon it and to renounce it; to claim and secure in my name any possessions on any of the estates or properties belonging to me and to act on my behalf in confiscations in the appropriate manner; to consider favorable sentences and to make agreements with the opposing party; to make appeals and suits, wherever it is possible by law; to see the trial through its conclusion; to charge and to recognize legal fees; in effect, to do everything that I could otherwise do, even if it is not explicitly listed or addressed and even though it concerns things of importance that would seem to require my presence. Insofar as my power must be given and transferred without limitation and legally, I give and transfer it to him with all of its consequences, attachments, and implications and with free and general administration. I further empower him to transfer the said power of attorney to other person or persons according to his best judgment and to revoke this transferal. I free him and them from all responsibility and liquidate as a guarantee all goods, tributes, interests, and estates that are appropriate for that purpose, in the present or the future, and mobile or fixed.

In order to certify the foregoing, I have signed it with my name. Completed on the sixth day of the month of February of the year 1570. The following witnesses were present during its drafting: the reverend fray Don Marcos García and fray Diego Ortiz, as well as Don Pablo Huallpa Yupanqui and Don Martín Cusi Guaman and Don Gaspar Sulca Yanaq.

I, Martín de Pando, notary in the service of the very illustrious governor, the licentiate Don Castro, certify the truth of the above declaration and the fact that the said Inca Don Diego de Castro has given this power of attorney to the said licentiate Don Castro, formerly governor of these kingdoms. In order to certify this, I place the signature in his name Don Diego de Castro below, as it appears the original below.

Don Diego de Castro Titu Cusi Yupanqui.
Witnessed by fray Marcos García.
Witnessed by fray Diego Ortiz.
As certification of the truth I place here my seal.
Martín de Pando, commissioned notary.

Notes

1. By traditional chronologies of modern Inca historiography, Huayna Capac was the eleventh ruler of the Inca Empire and lived from 1493–1526 (?); see Introduction.

2. Manco Inca Yupanqui (1516–1544), one of Huayna Capac's sons, ruled from 1533 to his death.

3. On Titu Cusi's assertion of primogeniture, see the Introduction.

4. Ruler of Tahuantinsuyu from 1471–1493.

5. Most historians today agree that Huayna Capac's intended heir was Ninan Coyoche, who died shortly before Huayna Capac died. Urteaga says that Huascar was Huayna Capac's preferred second choice (see Urteaga, *Relación de la Conquista del Perú*, 5–6, n. 2).

6. One Spanish league is about 3.4 miles or 5.5 km.

7. At the time when the Spaniards arrived in Peru, Cuzco was governed by Quisquis, one of Atahuallpa's generals, who ruled the town in Atahuallpa's name and persecuted the members of Huascar's family. When Atahuallpa was imprisoned by the Spaniards at Cajamarca, Quisquis left Cuzco for the part of the empire known as Chinchaysuyu and Cuzco was governed by Huascar's remaining brothers until the Spanish arrival in the city. Pizarro had first crowned Topa Huallpa, another one of Huayna Capac's sons. Only when Topa Huallpa died did the Spaniards crown Manco Inca (see Introduction; also Urteaga, *Relación de la Conquista del Perú*, 8, n. 4).

8. The word "bastard" appears to refer to an Andean logic of legitimacy here. This claim is controversial (see Introduction).

9. Manuscript (ff 133): *Teqse Viraochan*; Academia Mayor de la lengua Quechua, *Diccionario Quechua-Español-Quechua* (Qosqo: Municipalidad

de Qosqo, 1995) (henceforth Academia Mayor), 620: *Teqsi Wiraqocha*. Martín de Pando's *Viracocha*[n] in the manuscript corresponds with the orthography of fray Domingo de Santo Tomás's 1560 bilingual (Quechua/Spanish) dictionary (henceforth ST) (369). *Teqse* is not in ST. Pierre Duviols argues that the idea of Viracocha as a "creator god" is a European imposition, the result of missionaries' attempt to give a "Christian mask" to indigenous deities ("Los nombres quechua de Viracocha, supuesto 'Dios Creador' de los evangelizadores," *Allpanchis: revista del Instituto de Pastoral Andina* 10 (1977): 53); he translates the concept of *Tecsi Viracocha* as "father of the people, master who knew and knows how to order the world" ("Los nombres," 60).

10. Ladrón's translation for Spanish *trueno* is *qhaqy* (Laura Ladrón de Guevara de Cuadros, *Diccionario Quechua: Ingles, quechua, español: Español, quechua, ingles: Quechua, ingles, español* [Lima: Editorial Brasa, 1998] [henceforth Ladrón], 281). Martín de Pando's orthography—*yllapas* in the manuscript—corresponds here with ST: "*yllapa . . . trueno*" (301) but not with the grammatical rules for plural formation explained in Domingo de Santo Tomás *Gramática*.

11. *Chicha* is not originally a Quechua word but was imported by the Spaniards from the Caribbean and is, possibly for this reason, not listed by ST. See the Introduction.

12. As several commentators have pointed out (Urteaga, *Relación de la Conquista del Perú*, 9, n. 6), the chronology of events related by Titu Cusi here is not entirely reliable, as it seems to confound the first meeting between Atahuallpa and a small Spanish envoy at the baths of Cajamarca with the second one between Atahuallpa, Pizarro, and Vicente de Valverde in the main square on the following day (see also Hemming, *Conquest of the Incas*, 32–35).

13. As discussed in the Introduction, the claim that the mothers of Titu Cusi's warring uncles were "commoners" (meaning that they had no claim to be descendants of Manco Capac by their paternal line) follows a traditional Andean logic of succession but is factually controversial.

14. Manuscript (ff 134): *tomës* and *llamas;* singular forms: *tumi* and *llama* (Academia Mayor. 631, 262). Pando's orthography corresponds here with the singular form as rendered in ST—*tome*, "knife" (365) and *llama* (306), although not with the Quechua plural form, as explained in *Gramática*.

15. On the principle of "reciprocity" in Inca culture, see Constance Classen, *Inca Cosmology and the Human Body* (Salt Lake City: University of Utah Press, 1993), 1-2, 59-60.

16. The manuscript reads here *lazos* and *tumës,* rather than *tomës* as before.

17. *Usnu* in Academia Mayor (695); not in ST.

18. Hemming estimates the amount of Andean casualties at Cajamarca to be roughly 1,500 (*Conquest of the Incas,* 30).

19. This exchange may be part of a version particular to this narrative or the oral tradition kept by Manco Inca's family and followers. No other surviving records evidence the Spaniards' awareness of Manco Inca at this stage.

20. *çapay ynga* in manuscript (ff 140); not in ST but *sapay* in Academia Mayor (545).

21. Manuscript: *bienen por el viento* (ff 141).

22. As Felipe Guaman Poma de Ayala reports in his *Nueva corónica y buen gobierno* (codex péruvien illustré) (Paris: Institut d'ethnologie, 1936) (ff 303) lying was considered to be one of the cardinal sins in Inca codes of conduct, punishable with twenty lashes. As the reader will note, there is an emphasis throughout Titu Cusi's narrative on Spanish lies, especially with regard to the Spaniards' claim of being sons of Viracocha.

23. I have not been able to establish the identities of the two Spaniards mentioned here.

24. According to modern estimates, the treasure paid for Atahuallpa's ransom weighed 11 tons in gold and 26,000 pounds in silver (see Mark Burkholder and Lyman Johnson, *Colonial Latin America* [New York: Oxford University Press, 1994], 46).

25. This took place in 1533. This town is today known as Huánuco Viejo.

26. Manuscript (ff 138): *macho capitu. Macho* in Quechua means "old" or "great." *Capitu* seems to be derived from the Spanish *capitán* (captain). ST (313): *macho;* Academia Mayor (285): *machu.*

27. Most likely the reference here is to Spanish reals. John Hemming estimated that the ransom would have been worth roughly $13 million on the bullion market in 1970.

28. Manuscript (ff 139): *Apoës;* singular: ST (235): *Appó;* Ladrón (628): *Apu.*

29. Manuscript (ff 139): *hu Capay.*

30. This was on 26 July 1533.

31. I have found no corroborating evidence that Manco Inca played a role in the burning of Challcochima or even that his meeting between him and Pizarro ever took place. Hemming writes that Challcochima was burnt twice by the Spaniards—once for torture to extort gold (*Conquest of the Incas,* 70) and the second time to execute him for allegedly having plotted an uprising. This was on 13 November 1533 (109).

32. The person accompanying Manco Inca on this expedition was actually Hernando de Soto (Hemming, *Conquest of the Incas,* 126). De Soto would later be appointed governor of La Florida and die there during his exploration into North America; see Romero, "Biografía de Tito Cusi Yupanqui," 25, n. 30; also Luiselli, "Introducción," 45, n. 17.

33. Manuscript (ff 144): *Viracochas* and *Tecsi Viracochan.*

34. Manuscript (ff 145): *sapai ynga.*

35. A *taino* (Caribbean) word incorporated into American Spanish. It is a type of indigenous house, sometimes made of straw.

36. ST (266): *coya . . . reyna, o emperatriz, muger de emperador o de rey.* Academia Mayor (475): *qoya.* As pointed out in the Introduction, a woman's status of a *coya* rested not on that of her being a "wife" but rather on her claim to be a descendant of Manco Capac by her paternal line.

37. Manuscript (ff 145): *supay;* ST (99): *cúpay . . . demonio, bueno, o malo;* Academia Mayor (587): *supay.* As pointed out in the Introduction, cultural glosses of this kind must probably be attributed to Marcos García. In pre-Christian Andean culture, this word meant something closer to "mountain spirit." For a discussion of this concept, see Duviols, "Camaquen, Upani"; also ibid., "La destrucción." On the changes in Andean religious concepts resulting from European conquest and colonialism, see also Demarest, *Viracocha;* Adelaar, "A grammatical category"; Dedenbach-Salazar, "La terminología"; and ibid., ". . . luego."

38. Manuscript (ff 146): *Viracochas;* singular: ST (369): *Viracocha;* Academia Mayor (620): *Wiraqocha.*

39. Manuscript (ff 146): *Teqse Viracochan que quiere dezir dios;* see note 9.

40. For a good account of the background and history of the Pizarro brothers, see Varón Gabai, *Francisco Pizarro and His Brothers;* also Lockhart, *Men of Cajamarca.*

41. Urteaga (46) and Carillo (56) each transcribes here "confusion"; Millones, "confrission" (14); Regalado de Hurtado, "confussion" (29); and Luiselli, "contrición" (62). My own reading of the manuscript here (ff 192) corresponds with that of Regalado de Hurtado.

42. *Vila Oma* is not a personal name but a title for the highest priest, an office usually reserved for a brother, cousin, or uncle of the Inca.

43. Urteaga and Carillo each transcribe here "conquestardose," (47, 57, respectively); Millones, "conquestandosse" (14); Regalado de Hurtado, "conquistandosse" (29); and Luiselli, "contestándose" (63). My reading of the manuscript (ff 195) corresponds with that of Millones.

44. ST (238): *Atun . . . cosa grande;* Academia Mayor (147): *hatun.*

45. As pointed out in the Introduction, the suffix *-cona* (or *-kuna*) indicates the plural in Quechua, but the text is not consistent here (compare note 28, *apoes,* and note 72, *yanaconas*).

46. As Julien (*Reading Inca History,* 305, n. 13) points out, this woman may have been Francisca Ynguill, who later became the wife of Juan Pizarro; see also Introduction.

47. As pointed out in the Introduction, *coya* is not parallel to the European concept of "queen." Most likely, this gloss must again be attributed to Marcos García.

48. Lienhard notes here that this was probably the festival called *warakuq* or *warachikuq* ("to put on a loincloth or trousers for the covering of genitalia"). On this occasion, the orejones had their ears pierced so that the earplugs, the status symbol of the orejones, would be mounted (Lienhard, *Die Erschütterung der Welt: Ein Inka-Kónig berichted über den Kampf gegen die Spanier* [Augsburg, Germany: Bechtermünz Verlag, 1995], 167).

49. Urteaga (57), Carillo (69), Millones (18), and Regalado de Hurtado (37) all transcribe here *mas de mil,* but Luiselli (72) transcribes *más de diez mil.* My reading of the manuscript agrees with that of the majority (see ff 162)

50. Not in ST or Academia Mayor. Most likely *warakuq;* a participant in the initiation rite of the *wara,* a type of garment worn around the loin (see Lienhard, *Erschütterung,* 172).

51. Luiselli's transcription (73) adds here *se iban a lavar los pies* ("went to wash their feet"). Again, I have not found this to correspond to the manuscript (see ff 162), nor does it appear in any of the previous

transcriptions; see Urteaga (57), Carillo (69), Millones (18), and Regalado de Hurtado (37).

52. Not in ST or Academia Mayor. Most likely *yauri*, "needle" or "scepter" (see Lienhard, *Erschütterung*, 173).

53. I have not found any sources that shed light on the question of whether this dispatch that was sent *por la posta* was an oral message, in *quipu*, or already in writing.

54. This was 3 May 1536.

55. "[A]lçandoles la perneta" or "alzar la pierna" ("to lift a leg"), a gesture of mockery or jest, especially in a crude, provocative, or threatening way.

56. See the Introduction on some of the cultural and ideological ambiguities involving authorship in this text. While Titu Cusi was formally a convert to Christianity, it is somewhat implausible that he would praise what must doubtlessly be the Christian God in this context for intervening in the battle.

57. As Urteaga (*Relación de la Conquista del Perú* 70, n. 54) points out, the miraculous appearance of Santiago on a white horse, rushing to the aid of the Spaniards in battle, is commonplace in many Spanish chronicles of the conquest; and, as Luiselli (82, n. 39) points out, it is possible that we are here (and in other instances) dealing with an addition made by the Augustinian fray Marcos García. However, Guaman Poma de Ayala repeats it more than forty years later in his *Nueva corónica y buen gobierno* (see Introduction).

58. Although kissing the hands of a monarch was Spanish royal protocol, it may also have been practiced by the Inca. Miguel de Estete, for example, describes that when Challcochima greeted his lord Atahuallpa in Spanish captivity, he "went up to him with great reverence, weeping, and kissed him on the face, hands, and feet, and the other chiefs who had come with him did the same" (quoted in Hemming, *Conquest of the Incas*, 69).

59. By *Anti*, Titu Cusi meant the Inca province of the Antisuyu, not necessarily the Andes mountains.

60. The Spanish word used here in the manuscript is *documento* ("document") rather than the usual *parlamento* ("speech"); as Luiselli (87) has pointed out (among others), this choice of word highlights the official character of this chapter's content and *documento* must therefore be understood in the sense of *instrucción*.

61. Sacred objects and places, such as certain springs, boulders, hillsides, or mountains. Manuscript (ff 175): *guacas*; singular: ST (279) *Guaca*; Academia Mayor (706): *waka*.

62. Manuscript (ff 175): *villcas*; singular: ST (369): *Villca*; Academia Mayor (745): *willka*.

63. Not in ST. Lienhard glosses here *uywa*, "pet" (*Erschütterung* 172).

64. The Incas mummified the bodies of their dead rulers.

65. Actually Rodrigo Orgóñez, who would later side with Almagro against the Pizarros and who was finally assassinated by the Pizarros after Almagro's defeat.

66. This was in July 1537. See Introduction.

67. Pedro de Oñate, who aligned himself with Almagro against the Pizarros. He had previously met Manco Inca at Vilcabamba during an embassy on which he was sent by Almagro and was received hospitably by Manco Inca and seems to have been overall on friendly terms with him (see Hemming. *Conquest of the Incas,* 233).

68. Rabanto: probably Levantu or Llavantu, the ancient capital of the Chachapoya Indians. It exists today as a district called Levanto in the province of Chachapoyas in northern Peru. It is a great distance from Vitcos, and the journey would have involved crossing rugged terrain.

69. Manco Inca had apparently here already picked up Spanish fighting techniques, including the use of horses and lances.

70. The Guanca people had risen up several times against the Incas in pre-Hispanic times. When the Spaniards arrived in Peru, they readily allied themselves with them against the Inca armies commanded by Atahuallpa's generals.

71. In the vicinity of Huancayo.

72. Manuscript (180); not in ST; singular: Academia Mayor (759): *yana*. As noted in the Introduction, this form seems to hybridize Quechua with Castilian plural forms: *yana-cona* [or *-kuna*] *-s*.

73. Located in the province of Tayacaja, Huancavelica.

74. Normally the Incas incorporated such local deities into their pantheon. The characterization of its worship by the Guanca as idolatry may reflect a Christian influence.

75. Located at the Apurímac River.

76. Orgóñez.

77. This brother is otherwise known as Paullu.

78. These had been captured by the Spaniards in separate battles not recounted here.

79. The names of only five of those seven are known: Diego Méndez, Gómez Pérez, Cornejo, Monroy, and Francisco Barba (see Urteaga, *Relación de la Conquista del Perú*, 92, n. 80). It is no accident that Titu Cusi omits to mention the "crimes" for which these Spaniards were on the run. They had been involved in the murder of Francisco Pizarro, Manco Inca's old enemy. Although historians have often wondered about the "inexplicable trust" that Manco Inca placed in these men (Luiselli, "Introducción," 101), it is likely that their murder of Pizarro helped them to ingratiate themselves with Manco Inca.

80. *Herrón*: A kind of horseshoes, which must have been imported to Peru from Europe.

81. This was in 1544.

82. As noted in the Introduction, most modern historians agree that Manco Inca left the throne to Saire Topa, also a minor. However, some uncles ruled on his behalf until Saire Topa surrendered to the Spaniards in 1557 and went to Lima and ultimately to Cuzco. In 1560 Titu Cusi officially succeeded as ruler of the neo-Inca state at Vilcabamba.

83. Andrés Hurtado de Mendoza, Marquis de Cañete, was the third viceroy of Peru. His tenure was from 1556 to 1560.

84. A repartimiento was a grant of land and Indian tributaries associated with a certain obligations on the part of the grantee. Saire Topa died in 1560.

85. Juan Polo de Ondegardo was a corregidor, or municipal royal administrator, of Cuzco from 1558 to 1561 and from 1571 until his death in 1574. Martín de Pando was a mestizo and scribe who accompanied him and decided to stay in Vilcabamba after the embassy was complete. He later transcribed this text as dictated by Titu Cusi to fray Marcos García. Juan de Betanzos was a Spaniard who was married to Atahuallpa's sister-wife (and Francisco Pizarro's former mistress), Doña Angelina Yupanqui. He was fluent in Quechua. He had written a history of the Incas based on the traditions kept by his wife's family. See Introduction.

86. Given Titu Cusi's stay in Cuzco as a child and his documented curiosity about other aspects of European culture, his claim of ignorance with regard to Spanish attempts at proselytizing seems less than credible.

87. This took place in 1565.

88. On 24 August 1566.

89. Antonio de Vera was an Augustinian and the first to catechize Titu Cusi (in 1566).

90. This person was Atilano de Anaya, a rich and respected citizen of Cuzco who had come along as the guardian of Doña Beatriz, the daughter of Saire Topa, who owned large tracts of land as a result of her then deceased father's surrender. As related in the narrative, Titu Cusi had arranged for a marriage between Doña Beatriz and his son Quispe Titu as a part of the peace settlement.

91. Juan de Vivero was prior of the Augustinian convent of Cuzco. He catechized Titu Cusi in Vilcabamba in 1568 and also baptized Inca Tito.

92. Fray Marcos García, also a monk from the Augustinian order in Cuzco, is the translator of the present account. He had been charged with the instruction of Titu Cusi in 1569, the year after the latter's baptism. After catechizing many Inca noblemen, he was finally expelled from Vilcabamba, most likely for attempting to suppress the ancient custom of polygamy (see Urteaga, *Relación de la Conquista del Perú*, 106, n. 98).

93. This was September 1569.

94. Urteaga (107) and Carillo (128) transcribe here "ffecho," Millones (34) and Regalado de Hurtado (67) "fecho," and Luiselli (113) "hecho." In my opinion, the manuscript (ff 193) is amibiguous here, but the context would suggest "hecho" in the sense of "relatado," as in Martín de Pando's subsequent affirmation "lo relató y ordenó el dicho padre."

Bibliography

Works Cited

Academia Mayor de la lengua Quechua, *Diccionario Quechua-Español-Quechua*. Qosqo: Municipalidad de Qosqo, 1995.

Adelaar, Willem F.H. "La expresión de conceptos abstractos y generales en quechua: visión diacrónica." In *Andean Oral Traditions: Discourse and Literature/Tradiciones orales andinas: discurso y literatura*, ed. Margot Beyersdorff and Sabine Dedenbach-Salazar Sáenz, 1–20. Bonn: Bonner Amerikanistische Studien.

———. "A grammatical category for manifestations of the supernatural in early colonial Quechua." In *Language in the Andes*, ed. Peter Cole, Gabriella Hermon, and Mario Daniel Martín, 116–125. Newark: University of Delaware, 1994.

Adorno, Rolena, ed. *From Oral to Written Expression: Native Andean Chronicles of the Early Colonial Period.* Syracuse, NY: Maxwell School of Citizenship and Public Affairs, 1982.

Andrien, Kenneth. *Andean Worlds: Indigenous History, Culture, and Consciousness under Spanish Rule, 1532–1825.* Albuquerque: University of New Mexico Press, 2001.

Andrien, Kenneth, and Rolena Adorno, eds. *Transatlantic Encounters: Europeans and Andeans in the Sixteenth Century.* Berkeley: University of California Press, 1991.

Ascher, Marcia, and Robert Ascher. *Code of the Quipu.* Ann Arbor: University of Michigan Press, 1981.

Bauer, Ralph. "'EnCountering' Colonial Latin American Indian Chronicles: Guamán Poma de Ayala's History of the 'New' World." *American Indian Quarterly* 25:2 (Spring 2001): 274–312.

———. *The Cultural Geography of Colonial American Literatures: Empire, Travel, Modernity.* Cambridge: Cambridge University Press, 2003.

Betanzos, Juan de. *Narrative of the Incas.* Trans. and ed. Roland Hamilton and Dana Buchanan from the Palma de Mallorca manuscript. Austin: University of Texas Press, 1996.

Beyersdorff, Margot, and Sabine Dedenbach-Salazar Sáenz, eds. *Andean Oral Traditions: Discourse and Literature/Tradiciones Orales Andinas: Discurso y Literatura.* Bonn: Bonner Amerikanistische Studien, 1994.

Brading, David. *The First America: The Spanish Monarchy, Creole Patriots, and the Liberal State, 1492–1867.* Cambridge: Cambridge University Press, 1991.

Burkholder, Mark, and Lyman Johnson. *Colonial Latin America.* New York: Oxford University Press, 1994.

Cañizares-Esguerra, Jorge. *How to Write the History of the New World: Histories, Epistemologies, and Identities in the Eighteenth-Century Atlantic World.* Stanford, CA: Stanford University Press, 2001.

Chang-Rodríguez, Raquel. *La apropiación del signo: Tres cronistas indígenas del Perú.* Tempe: Center for Latin American Studies, Arizona State University, 1988.

———. *El discurso disidente: Ensayos de literatura colonial peruana.* Lima: Pontificia Universidad Católica del Perú, 1991.

———. *Violencia y subversion en la prosa colonial hispanoamericana, siglos xvi y xvii.* Potomac, MD: Studias Humanintatis, 1982.

———. "A Forgotten Indian Chronicle: Titu Cusi Yupanqui's Relación de la conquista del Peru." *Latin American Indian Literatures: A Review of American Indian Texts and Studies* 4 (1980): 87–95.

———. "Writing as Resistance: Peruvian History and the Relación of Titu Cussi Yupanqui." In R. Adorno, ed., *From Oral to Written Expression*, 41–64.

———. "Rebelión y religión en dos crónicas indígenas del Perú de ayer." *Revista de critica literaria latinoamericana* 14:28 (1988): 175–193.

Cieza de León, Pedro. *The Discovery and Conquest of Peru*. Ed. and trans. Alexandra Parma Cook and Noble David Cook. Durham: Duke University Press, 1998.

Classen, Constance. *Inca Cosmology and the Human Body*. Salt Lake City: University of Utah Press, 1993.

Cole, Peter, Gabriella Hermon, and Mario Daniel Martín, eds. *Language in the Andes*. Newark: University of Delaware, Latin American Studies Program, 1994.

D'Altroy, Terence. *The Incas*. Malden, MA, and Oxford, England: Blackwell Publishers, 2002.

Dedenbach-Salazar, Sabine. "El arte verbal de los textos quechuas de Huarochirí (Perú, siglo XVII) reflejado en la organización del discurso y en los medios estiisticos." In *Andean Oral Traditions: Discourse and Literature/Tradiciones orales andinas: discurso y literatura*, ed. Margot Beyersdorff and Sabine Dedenbach-Salazar Sáenz, 21–50. Bonn: Bonner Amerikanistische Studien, 1994.

———. ". . . luego no puedes negar que ay Dios Criador del mundo, pues tus Incas con no ser Christianos la alcanzaron a sauer, y lo llamaron Pachacamac": La lengua de la cristianización en los Sermones de los misterios de nuestra santa fe catolica de Fernando de Avendaño (1649). In *La lengua de la cristianización en Latinoamérica: Catequización e instrucción en lenguas amerindias/The Language of Christianization in Latin America: Catechisation and Instruction in Amerindian Languages*, ed. Sabine Dedenbach-Salazar and Lindsey Crickmay, 223–248. Markt Schwaben: Saurwein, 1999.

———. La terminología cristiana en textos quechuas de instrucción religiosa en el siglo XVI. In *Latin American Indian Literatures: Messages and Meanings*, ed. Mary Preuss, 195–209. Lancaster, CA: Labyrinthos, 1997.

Dedenbach-Salazar, Sabine, and Lindsey Crickmay, eds. *La lengua de la cristianización en Latinoamérica: Catequización e instrucción en lenguas amerindias/The Language of Christianization in Latin America: Catechisation and Instruction in Amerindian Languages*. Markt Schwaben: Saurwein, 1999.

Demarest, Arthur. *Viracocha: The Nature and Antiquity of the Andean High God*. Cambridge, MA: Peabody Museum of Archaeology and Ethnology, Harvard University, 1991.

Duviols, Pierre. "Camaquen, Upani: un concept animiste des anciens peruviens" *Amerikanistische Studien I. Festschrift für Hermann Trimborn anlässlich seines 75. Geburtstages = Estudios americanistas I. Libro jubilar en homenaje a Hermann Trimborn con motivo de su septuagésimoquinto aniversario*. Ed. Roswith Hartmann, and Udo Oberem (Collectanea instituti Anthropos, 20). St. Augustin: Haus Völker und Kulturen, Anthropos-Institut, 1978. 132–144.

———. "La destrucción de las religiones andinas: conquista y colonia." *Historia general* 9. México: Universidad nacional autónoma de México, Instituto de investigaciones históricas. 441–459.

———. *La Lutte contre les réligions autocthones dans le Pérou colonial*. Lima: Institut Français d'Études Andines, 1972.

———. "Los nombres quechua de Viracocha, supuesto 'Dios Creador' de los evangelizadores." *Allpanchis: revista del Instituto de Pastoral Andina* 10 (1977): 53–64.

Espinoza Soriano, Waldemar. *Destrucción del imperio de los incas: la rivalidad política y señorial de los curacazgos andinos*. Lima: Ediciones Retablo de Papel, 1973.

Garcilaso de la Vega, el Inca. *Obras Completas del Inka Garcilaso de la Vega*. Edición y estudio preliminar de P. Carmelo Saenz de Santa Maria. t. 133. Biblioteca de Autores Españoles desde la formación del lenguaje hasta nuestros días. Madrid: Real Academia Española, 1960.

González Echevarría, Roberto. "Humanismo, Retórica y las Crónicas de la Conquista." In *Isla a su Vuelo Fugitiva: Ensayos Criticos sobre Literatura Hispanoamericana*, 9–26. Madrid: José Porrúa Turanzas, S.A. 1983.

———. *Myth and Archive: A Theory of Latin American Narrative*. Cambridge: Cambridge University Press, 1990.

―――. "The Life and Adventures of Cipion: Cervantes and the Picaresque." *Diacritics* 9:11 (1980): 15–26.

Guaman Poma de Ayala, Felipe. *Nueva corónica y buen gobierno* (codex péruvien illustré). Paris: Institut d'ethnologie, 1936.

Guillén Guillén, Edmundo. *Versión inca de la conquista*. Lima: Editorial Milla Batres, 1974.

―――. "Titu Cussi Yupanqui y su tiempo: El estado imperial inca y su trágico final, 1572." *Historia y Cultura* 13–14. Lima: Museo Nacional de Historia, 1981. 61–99.

Hanke, Lewis. *The Spanish Struggle for Justice in the Conquest of America*. Philadelphia: University of Pennsylvania Press, 1965.

Harrison, Regina. *Signs, Songs, and Memory in the Andes: Translating Quechua Language and Culture*. Austin: University of Texas Press, 1989.

Hemming, John. *The Conquest of the Incas*. New York: Harcourt Brace Jovanovich, 1970.

The Huarochirí Manuscript, a Testament of Ancient and Colonial Andean Religion, ed. Frank Salomon and George Urioste. Austin: University of Texas Press, 1991.

Jákfalvi-Leiva, Susana. "De la voz a la escritura: La Relación de Titu Cusi (1570)." *Revista de Crítica Literaria Latinoamericana*. 19:37 (1993): 259–277.

Julien, Catherine. *Reading Inca History*. Iowa City: University of Iowa Press, 2000.

Kubler, George. "The Neo-Inca State (1537–1572)." *The Hispanic American Historical Review* 27:2 (1947): 189–200.

Ladrón de Guevara de Cuadros, Laura. *Diccionario Quechua: Ingles, quechua, español: Español, quechua, ingles: Quechua, ingles, español*. Lima: Editorial Brasa, 1998.

Lara, Jesús. *La poesía quechua*. Mexico City: Fondo de Cultura Económica, 1979.

Lienhard, Martin. "La epica incaica en tres textos coloniales (Juan de Betanzos, Titu Cusi Yupanqui, el Ollantay)." *Lexis* 9:1 (1985): 61–80.

―――, ed. *Die Erschütterung der Welt: Ein Inka-König berichtet über den Kampf gegen die Spanier*. Augsburg, Germany: Bechtermünz Verlag, 1995.

Lockhart, James. *The Men of Cajamarca: Social and Biographical Study of the First Conquerors of Peru*. Austin: University of Texas Press, 1972.

————. *Spanish Peru, 1532–1560*. Madison: University of Wisconsin Press, 1994.

Lohmann Villena, Guillermo. "El Inca Titu Cusi Yupanqui y su entrevista con el oidor Matienzo (1565)." *Mercurio Peruano* 66 (1941): 4–18.

Luiselli, Alessandra. "Introducción." In *Instrucción del Inca don Diego de Castro Titu Cusi Yupanqui*, ed. Alessandra Luiselli. Mexico: Universidad Nacional Autónoma de México, 2001.

Mackehenie, Carlos. "Apuntes sobre Don Diego e Castro Titu Cusi Yupanqui." *Revista Histórica* 3 (1909): 371–390.

MacCormack, Sabine. "Pachacuti: Miracles, Punishments, and Last Judgment: Visionary Past and Prophetic Future in Early Colonial Peru." *The American Historical Review* 93:4 (October 1988): 960–1006.

————. *Religion in the Andes: Vision and Imagination in Early Colonial Peru*. Princeton, NJ: Princeton University Press, 1991.

MacLeod, Murdo. "The relaciones de Méritos y Servicios and their Historical and Political Interpretation." In *The Book in the Americas*, ed. Julie Greer Johnson. Providence, RI: John Carter Brown Library, 1987.

Mannheim, Bruce. *The Language of the Inka since the European Invasion*. Austin: University of Texas Press, 1991.

Mignolo, Walter. "El Métatexto Historiográfico y la Historiografía Indiana." *MLN* 96:2 (1981): 358–402.

————. "Cartas, crónicas y relaciones del descubrimiento y la conquista." In *Historia de la literatura hispanoamericana, época colonial* ed. Luis Iñigo Madrigal, 57–116. Madrid: Ediciones Cátedra, 1982.

Millones, Luis. "Introducción." *Ynstrucción del Ynga Don Diego de Castro Titu Cusi Yupangui*. Edición facsímil de Luis Millones. Lima: Ediciones El Virrey, 1985.

Moseley, Michael. *The Incas and Their Ancestors*. London: Thames and Hudson, 1992.

Murra, John. *El Mundo Andino: población, medio ambiente y economía*. Lima: Pontifica Universidad Católica del Perú, 2002.

Niles, Susan. *The Shape of Inca History: Narrative and Architecture in an Andean Empire*. Iowa City: University of Iowa Press, 1999.

Ocampo, Baltasar de. "The Execution of the Inca Tupac Amaru." *History of the Incas by Sarmiento de Gamboa and The Execution of the Inca*

Tupac Amaru by Captain Baltasar de Ocampo. Trans. and ed. Sir Clements Markham. London: Hakluyt Society, 1907, 203–247.

Patterson, Thomas. *Inca Empire: The Formation and Disintegration of a Precapitalist State.* New York: St. Martin's Press, 1991.

Pérez, Julio Calvo. *Pragmática y Gramática del Quechua Cuzqueño.* Cuzco: Centro de Estudios Regionales Andinos Bartolomé de Las Casas, 1993.

Pagden, Anthony. *The Fall of Natural Man: The American Indian and the Origins of Comparative Ethnology.* Cambridge: Cambridge University Press, 1982.

Pizarro, Pedro. "Relación del desubrimiento y conquista de los reinos del Perú (1571)." In *Crónicas del Perú,* 5, 159–242. Biblioteca de Autores Españoles, no. 168. Madrid: Atlas, 1963–1965.

Rama, Angel. *The Lettered City.* Ed. and trans. John Charles Chasteen. Durham: Duke University Press, 1996.

Ramírez, Susan Elizabeth. *The World Upside Down: Cross-Cultural Contact and Conflict in Sixteenth-Century Peru.* Stanford: Stanford University Press, 1996.

Regalado de Hurtado, Liliana. "La relación de Titu Cussi Yupanqui. Valor de un testimonio tardío." *Histórica* 5:1 (1981): 45–62.

———. "Introducción." In Titu Cusi Yupanqui's *Instrucción al licenciado don Lope García de Castro* (1570), ed. Liliana Regalado de Hurtado. Lima: Fondo Editorial de la Pontificia Universidad Católica del Perú, 1992.

———. *El inca Titu Cusi Yupanqui y su tiempo: los incas de Vilcabamba y los primeros cuarenta años del dominio español.* Lima: Pontificia Universidad Católica del Perú, Fondo Editorial, 1997.

Romero, Carlos. "Biografía de Tito Cusi Yupanqui." In Diego de Castro Titu Cusi Yupanqui's *Relación de la Conquista del Perú y hechos del Inca Manco II,* ed. Horacio H. Urteaga, xxii–xxiv. Collección de Libros y Documentos relativos a la Historia del Perú, t. II. Lima: Imprenta y Librería San Martí y Compañía, 1916.

Rostworowski de Diez Canseco, María. *History of the Inca Realm.* Trans. Harry B. Iceland. Cambridge: Cambridge University Press, 1999.

Salomon, Frank. "Chronicles of the Impossible: Notes on Three Peruvian Indigenous Historians. In *From Oral to Written Expression: Native Andean Chronicles of the Early Colonial Period,* ed. Rolena Adorno.

Syracuse, NY: Maxwell School of Citizenship and Public Affairs, 1982, 9–40.

———. "Introduction." In *The Huarochirí Manuscript, a Testament of Ancient and Colonial Andean Religion,* ed. Frank Salomon and George Urioste, 1–38. Austin: University of Texas Press, 1991.

Santa Cruz Pachacuti, Juan de. "Relación de antigüedades deste reyno del Pirú." In *Tres relaciones de antigüedades peruanas,* ed. Marcos Jiménez de la Espada, 23–328. Madrid: Imprenta y Fundición de M. Tello, 1879.

Santo Tomás, Domingo de. *Lexicon o vocabulario de la lengua general del Peru* [1560]. Edición facsimilar por Raúl Porras Barrenechea. Lima: Edición del instituto de Historia, 1951.

———. *Gramática o arte de la lengua general de los indios de los reynos del Perú* [1561]. Edición facsimilar por Raúl Porras Barrenechea. Lima: Edición del instituto de Historia, 1951.

Sarmiento de Gamboa, Pedro. "History of the Incas." In *History of the Incas by Sarmiento de Gamboa and The Execution of the Inca Tupac Amaru by Captain Baltasar de Ocampo.* Trans. and ed., Sir Clements Markham. London: Hakluyt Society, 1907.

Spalding, Karen. *Huarochirí: An Andean Society under Inca and Spanish Rule.* Stanford: Stanford University Press, 1984.

Stern, Steve. *Peru's Indian Peoples and the Challenge of Spanish Conquest: Huamanga to 1640.* Madison: University of Wisconsin Press, 1993.

Urton, Gary. *The Social Life of Numbers: A Quechua Ontology of Numbers and Philosophy of Arithmetic.* Austin: University of Texas Press, 1997.

———. *The History of a Myth.* Austin: University of Texas Press, 1990.

———. "From Knots to Narratives: Reconstructing the Art of Historical Record Keeping in the Andes from Spanish Transcriptions of the Inka Khipus." *Ethnohistory* 45:3 (1998): 409–438.

Varón Gabai, Rafael. *Francisco Pizarro and His Brothers: The Illusion of Power in Sixteenth-century Peru.* Trans. Javier Flores Espinoza. Norman: University of Oklahoma Press, 1997.

Veber, Hanne. "Ashánika Messianism." *Current Anthropology* 44:2 (April 2003): 183–211.

Verdesio, Gustavo. "Traducción y contrato en la obra de Titu Cusi Yupanqui." *Bulletin of Hispanic Studies* 72 (1995): 403–412.

Wachtel, Nathan. *The Vision of the Vanquished: The Spanish Conquest of Peru through Indian Eyes, 1530–1570.* Trans. Ben and Siân Reynolds. New York: Barnes and Noble, 1977.

Editions and Translations of
Titu Cusi Yupanqui's Account

Relación de la Conquista del Perú y hechos del Inca Manco II. Ed. Horacio H. Urteaga, Collección de Libros y Documentos relativos a la Historia del Perú, t. II. Lima: Imprenta y Librería San Martí y Compañía, 1916.

Relación de la Conquista del Perú. Titu Cusi Yupanqui. Edición de Francisco Carillo. Lima: Ediciones de la Biblioteca Universitaria, 1973.

"Titu Cusi's account of Manco's rebellion." In *New Iberian World: A Documentary History of the Discovery and Settlement of Latin America to the Early 17th Century,* ed. John H. Parry and Robert G. Keith, 134–145. New York: Times Books, Hector & Rose, 1984.

"Titu Cusi's Account of Manco's Flight to Vitcos." In *New Iberian World: A Documentary History of the Discovery and Settlement of Latin America to the Early 17th Century,* ed. John H. Parry and Robert G. Keith, 268–272. New York: Times Books, Hector & Rose, 1984.

Ynstrucción del Ynga Don Diego de Castro Titu Cusi Yupangui. Edición facsímil de Luis Millones. Lima: Ediciones El Virrey, 1985.

Instrucción al licenciado don Lope García de Castro (1570). Ed. Liliana Regalado de Hurtado. Lima: Fondo Editorial de la Pontificia Universidad Católica del Perú, 1992.

Die Erschütterung der Welt: Ein Inka-König berichtet über den Kampf gegen die Spanier. Ed. and trans. Martin Lienhard. Augsburg: Bechtermünz Verlag, 1995.

Instrucción del Inca don Diego de Castro Titu Cusi Yupanqui. Ed. Alessandra Luiselli. Mexico: Universidad Nacional Autónoma de México, 2001.

Glossary of Quechua and Spanish Terms Appearing in the Text

Unless otherwise noted, terms are Quechua in origin.

Anti. Inhabitants of the *Antisuyu.*

Antisuyu. One of the four parts of the Inca Empire, located in a south-easterly direction from Cuzco, in the subtropical slopes of the Andes.

Apo. Lord, master.

Audiencia (Spanish). High court and colonial agency directly answerable to the Crown.

Bohío (taíno, Haiti). House, hut, or building.

Cañari. An ethnic group living in the southern part of present-day Ecuador and famous for their archery.

Chachapoya. An ethnic group living on the eastern slopes of the Andes in northern Peru

Chinchaysuyu. One of the four parts of the Inca empire, located to the northwest of Cuzco, in present-day northern Peru, Ecuador, and Colombia.

Cuntisuyu. One of the four parts of the Inca empire, located to the southwest of Cuzco, including parts of present-day Arequipa and Ayacucho.

Collasuyu. One of the four parts of the Inca empire, located to the south of Cuzco toward Lake Titicaca, including parts of present-day Bolivia, northwest Argentina, and Chile.

Corregidor (Spanish). Holder of high official imperial office with judicative and executive powers, ruling a district called a *corregimiento.*

Coya. Title for a female member of the Inca nobility who could claim descent from Manco Capac by her paternal line.

Huaca. Sacred thing or space in Inca culture.

Oidor (Spanish). Judge serving in the royal *audiencia.*

Repartimiento (Spanish). Royal grant of native tribute labor to an individual.

Supai. Supernatural being, good or evil.

Tahuantinsuyu. The Inca empire and world, made up of four parts: *Cuntisuyu, Chinchaysuyu, Collasuyu,* and *Antisuyu.*

Tecsi Viracocha. Original godhead.

Tome (tume). A ceremonial knife with a half-round blade generally made of copper.

Usnu. The Inca's ceremonial seat and a symbol of his dignity and power.

Villca. A sacred object in Inca religion.

Viracocha. The name for an androgynous deity used in many parts of the Andes.

Yanacona. Servants dedicated to powerful person or deity.

Yunca. Ethnic group inhabiting the tropical or subtropical valleys and coastal regions.

Index

Barba, Francisco, 125, 147n79
Beatriz (daughter of Saire Topa), 15,
53n18, 131, 147n90
Betanzos, Juan de, 19, 26, 37, 43,
55n29, 129, 146n85
Biblioteca del Monasterio de San
Lorenzo del Escorial, 12, 48, 50

Cachicachi, 29
Cajamarca, 1, 4, 6, 9, 18, 51n4, 59, 60,
61, 62, 63, 64, 65, 67, 74, 77, 89, 91,
107, 139n7, 140n12, 141n18, 142n40
Calancha, Antonio de, 17
Callca, 103, 104, 105
Cañari, 108
Cañizares Esguerra, Jorge, 31
Capi, 71, 72
Caribbean, 2, 42, 140n11, 142n35
Carillo, Francisco, 49
Carlos V (Charles V, King of Spain and
Holy Roman Emperor), 24, 73, 128
Carlos Inca, 13
Carmen Martín Rubio, María del, 49
Carmenga, 29, 104, 105
Castilian, 13; and Andeans, 13
Castro Titu Cusi Yupanqui, Diego, 1,
10, 11, 25, 26, 27, 30, 31, 32, 35, 36,
37, 38, 39, 40, 41, 42, 43, 48, 49,
50n1, 51n3, 53nn16, 18, 53–54n20,
54n26, 55n29, 57, 114, 126, 128,
135, 136, 139, 139n3, 140nn12, 13,
141n22, 142n32, 144nn56, 59,
146nn79, 82, 85, 86, 147nn89, 90,
91, 92; his account, textual history,
12; and alphabetical writing, 18–20;
biography, 12–23; dress, 17; gives
power of attorney to García de
Castro, 136–138; his language, 12–
14; his legitimacy as ruler, 37–41;
makes peace with Spaniards and
converts to Christianity, 128–135;
negotiations with Spaniards, 16; and

non-alphabetical traditions, 20–21,
28–30, 35; poetics of narrative, 17–
18; relationship with the licentiate
García de Castro, 15; relationship
with Marcos García, 16; religious
policy, 15–16; requests that his
narrative be written down and
appeals to García de Castro to
present his narrative to Philip II,
135–136; rhetorical purpose of his
account, 32, 35–36; rule of
Vilcabamba, 16–17; takes charge of
Vilcabamba, 10; transmission
history of his account, 48–50
Chachapoya (ethnic group), 108, 118,
145n68
Challcochima, 69, 70, 89, 91, 141n31,
144n58
Chanca, 40
Chang-Rodríguez, Raquel, 32
Chinchaysuyu, 2, 29, 77, 103, 105, 139
Chuquichaca, 15, 132
Cieza de León, Pedro de, 26, 37, 49
Classen, Constance, 20, 42
Collasuyu, 2, 29, 77, 103, 105
Condorcanqui Topa Amaru II, José
Gabriel, 11
Conoc, 61
Coriatao, 29, 103, 105, 124
Cortés, Hernando, 2
Count of Nieva. *See* López de Zuñiga,
Diego
coya, 25, 36–37
Coyllas, 103
Cuenca, González de, Gregorio. *See*
González de Cuenca, Gregorio
Cuillas, 29, 105
Cullcomayo, 111, 114
Cuntisuyu, 2, 77, 103, 105
Cura Oclo, 40–41, 75, 118, 123
Curi Huallpa, 29, 105
Cusi Guaman, Martín, 138